T0339724

WHAT TO EXPECT
WHEN YOU'RE EXPECTED TO
TEACH GIFTED STUDENTS

WHAT TO EXPECT
WHEN YOU'RE EXPECTED TO
TEACH GIFTED
STUDENTS

A GUIDE TO THE CELEBRATIONS, SURPRISES, QUIRKS, AND QUESTIONS IN YOUR FIRST YEAR TEACHING GIFTED LEARNERS

KARI LOCKHART

Routledge
Taylor & Francis Group

NEW YORK AND LONDON

Library of Congress Cataloging-in-Publication Data

Names: Lockhart, Kari, 1985- author.
Title: What to expect when you're expected to teach gifted students: a guide to the celebrations, surprises, quirks, and questions in your first year teaching gifted learners / Kari Lockhart.
Description: Waco, TX : Prufrock Press Inc., [2019] | Includes bibliographical references. | Summary: "What to Expect When You're Expected to Teach Gifted Students" is a practical, easy-to-read guide to what teachers may experience during their first year teaching gifted students. From the joys and surprises to the frustrations and questions, this book addresses specific topics related to gifted education, including students' social-emotional needs, choosing appropriate curricular materials, working with parents and families, advocating for gifted and advanced programming, and continued professional learning. In each chapter, readers dive into issues that are frequently cited as challenges for new gifted teachers and emerge equipped with real-world advice, resources, and strategies to build a successful classroom that meets the needs of high-ability students. This book is perfect for any teacher new to the field of gifted education"-- Provided by publisher.
Identifiers: LCCN 2019032643 | ISBN 9781618219077 (paperback) | ISBN 9781618219084 (ebook) | ISBN 9781618219268 (epub)
Subjects: LCSH: Gifted children--Education (Elementary)--United States. | Teachers of gifted children--United States.
Classification: LCC LC3993.22 .L62 2019 | DDC 371.95--dc23
LC record available at https://lccn.loc.gov/2019032643

First published in 2019 by Prufrock Press Inc.

Published in 2021 by Routledge
605 Third Avenue, New York, NY 10017
2 Park Square, Milton Park, Abingdon, Oxon OX14 4RN

Routledge is an imprint of the Taylor & Francis Group, an informa business.

Cover design by Micah Benson and layout design by Raquel Trevino

ISBN: 9781032142043 (hbk)
ISBN: 9781618219077 (pbk)

DOI: 10.4324/9781003239529

DEDICATION

I want to express my gratitude to all of the uniquely talented gifted teachers, leaders, and scholars with whom I have had the pleasure of working—without the opportunity for collaboration with you all, this book would not have been possible.

TABLE OF
CONTENTS

INTRODUCTION

As you move through your first year teaching gifted students, you will experience struggles (both expected and unexpected), successes, and surprises that can only arise in a gifted classroom. Although the first year you spend teaching (period) might be the most difficult, your first year in gifted education presents a whole new set of unique challenges. If you go into the gifted classroom thinking that the school year will be easy because you have the "good" kids, you will very quickly learn that high ability does not equal zero behavior issues, nor does it mean that the students will be free of academic difficulties. You will (routinely) also not know the answers to the questions students pose, and you may frequently find yourself going back to the drawing board to completely restructure a lesson based on your preassessments or unexpected student feedback. Teaching gifted students may mean that you redefine the way you see yourself as a teacher altogether. You may encounter student and parent needs that are very different from that to which you were accustomed. You may be facing a blank slate in terms of planning learning and designing content.

Even for an experienced teacher, the first year teaching gifted students might be like Day 1 of your first-ever teaching job all over again.

Along with some of the bumpier roads you will travel as you transition into teaching gifted classes, there are many exciting positive experiences to anticipate. You will get to see the students whom you routinely passed in the hallway or the lunchroom, or even some of your own former students, in a new light. In this light, they will show you their gifts, talents, interests, and struggles in ways that you may not have encountered or expected. You may recognize some of yourself or your own children in these students and view teaching through a new lens. You will undoubtedly find the opportunity to grow in your profession and do meaningful work for students and families in the gifted classroom. With the trials of teaching come the joys of teaching, just like in any classroom, but the ways in which you live these celebrations and frustrations may be unlike other experiences you have had in the classroom.

There will be many "uh-oh" moments, and that is completely okay. You give your students permission to make mistakes, recognize what went wrong, fix the mistakes, and then make more mistakes. You know that this means that they are learning. You are learning, too, and learning cannot occur without teacher uh-ohs, failures, and misses. As many learning moments as you will have, you will also experience aha moments, celebrations with students, and the chance to grow as a professional. Your job as a gifted teacher is to help meet students' needs in areas with which you may be unfamiliar, and at times your students' needs may seem to be at odds with one another. Gifted students are precocious, are complex, and have intensities that require accelerated

> **TEACHING GIFTED STUDENTS MAY MEAN THAT YOU REDEFINE THE WAY YOU SEE YOURSELF AS A TEACHER.**

and enriched learning opportunities (VanTassel-Baska, 2003). Gifted students benefit both academically and socioemotionally from their enrichment experiences (Kim, 2016). This still means that some of these students need additional academic support or intervention in certain areas, and this can be a tough pill to swallow for students used to having all of the right answers. Questions of self-efficacy, motivation, and performance versus potential are ones that gifted learners and teachers face regularly. You, as the teacher, can tackle these unique needs and facilitate the types of learning that help these students to develop the talents and skills needed for them to be fulfilled and successful. This task can seem daunting, but it can also be a wonderful growth experience for you as an individual and an educator.

WHERE DO I BEGIN?

You may approach this book as someone just assigned to teach a gifted class, or you may be reading this as someone who just finished his or her first year teaching gifted students. If you have had some experience in the gifted classroom, your initial expectations and actual experiences may not have lined up completely (or at all). If you are brand new to this, you may have no idea what to expect. Regardless of where you are beginning, I want to address some common issues teachers often struggle with when starting off teaching gifted learners. Do any of these thoughts or feelings look familiar to you?

- "I just got assigned to teach gifted classes. I know that we have a gifted and talented program, but I don't know much beyond that. What does *gifted* mean around here?"
- "The teacher before me left so many disjointed resources behind. What do I make of all of this stuff?"
- "The year has started, and all of a sudden I am not on a team anymore. I feel like I'm stranded on an island."
- "I thought I had so much freedom, and I could finally teach what I wanted to students who were excited to

learn! My lessons fell flat and my kids didn't engage, so now I'm not even sure how to move forward."

- "Sometimes a class of nine feels like a class of 29 . . . even in gifted classes, the kids' abilities are all over the place!"
- "I'm drowning in parent e-mails and phone calls. How do I balance making the parents happy and taking the time to plan what's best for my students?"
- "It feels like gifted programming is the lowest priority in our school. I'm constantly getting told 'no' or forgotten about completely. How can I advocate for this service and my students?"

If you have experienced these thoughts or questions, you are not alone. Many educators new to the gifted classroom share similar feelings when starting out the year. I can say with complete certainty that I have had all of these thoughts and feelings, and some of these problems and doubts persist over time. I would love to tell you to embrace the uncertainty and be ready to go wherever this teaching ride takes you, but that would not be helpful or practical. Starting out, the best you can do is build professional knowledge, try your best to be proactive, and try to view your experiences as learning opportunities. This book is intended to support teachers new to the gifted education classroom by focusing on targeted areas that are frequently challenges for new gifted teachers. Each chapter will identify the major issues associated with a specific topic, seek to provide guidance and resources, and make suggestions about strategies for developing solutions unique to the needs of your classrooms and campuses.

Teaching is extremely important work. Good teaching results in lifelong learning, and this year will be an experience that helps you to learn and build your professional skills. A new job can be a great teacher if you continually seek answers, ways to grow, and opportunities to learn. Whether you teach gifted for one year or 20, the students, the classroom, and the challenges have the potential to build your skills, broaden your insights, and make career-changing connections.

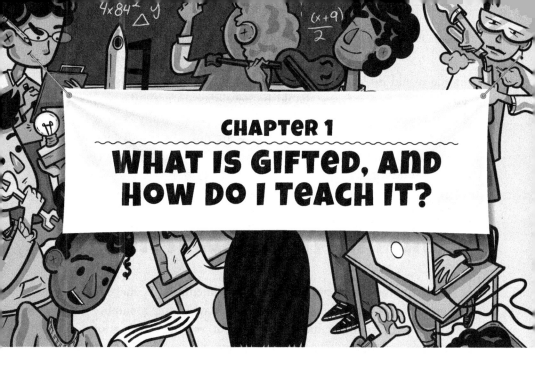

CHAPTER 1
WHAT IS GIFTED, AND HOW DO I TEACH IT?

Identifying effective instructional frameworks, curricula, and appropriate resources can be a daunting task to a teacher new to gifted education. As in any successful learning environment, these are the keys to creating, sustaining, and evaluating high-quality instruction. If you are starting from the ground up, so to speak, in terms of crafting a program that meets your students' needs, this is a huge task. It requires knowledge of gifted education theory, as well as skillful choice and development of curriculum materials, to make good choices regarding the allocation of valuable resources. You can quickly become overwhelmed. This is a challenge that new and seasoned teachers alike approach with similar levels of intimidation—if you are feeling like this job is too big and has too few parameters, you are not alone. This chapter begins the book with some basic understandings in terms of curriculum and instructional design from which you can move forward.

Although it might seem overly simplistic, I will use the metaphor of building a house throughout this chapter to help illustrate strategies for understanding, developing, and refining instructional gifted practices. If one is to go through the time, trouble, and expense of building a home, it is reasonable to believe that he or she would do so to have a well-constructed and long-lasting structure. Gifted services should be developed in a similar way. Educators want to create well thought out and carefully crafted learning opportunities for students that are not a one-and-done experience. If you seek to develop such a structure, the first step is laying a solid foundation.

WHAT IS MY FOUNDATION?

Perhaps you have never taught gifted students at all, and this assignment is a brand-new challenge. Or, maybe after a number of years in the general education classroom, you are looking for a different experience. Regardless of where you are starting out, understanding the "what" and "why" behind gifted services in your school is the most important first step to planning. These are the foundational supports that will allow you to build your decision-making skills as a new gifted teacher.

Unlike general education classrooms, in which parameters are often developed by district-selected resources and guidelines, the classroom of the gifted teacher is many times the Wild West in terms of what is taught and how. The curriculum in the gifted classroom might seem nebulous or piecemeal, without any real objectives or direction. Lacking a clear instructional progression or articulated outcomes, how can you know that you are following through with instruction that will help your students grow? Unless there is a distinct vision or expectation for gifted education in your school, this is a difficult question to answer.

DEFINING GIFTED

Understanding the "what" behind gifted education on your campus or in your district is the best place to begin seeking direction for designing instruction. Do you know, specifically, how your school defines gifted? Is there a distinct vision of what it means to be gifted in your school? If you are not sure, board policy documents, as well as your school's student or parent handbooks, are the most reasonable places to start. Your school's gifted program may have a standalone document outlining services, too. You may have a district coordinator or instructional leader on your campus who can help you learn more about how your school defines giftedness and for what purpose(s) your organization serves gifted students. In the case that there is no clear definition of gifted for your school, this could be a good opportunity to collaborate with your leadership team to create or hone a vision. This might seem like a very basic step, but pinning down a clear definition helps to provide a solid foundation on which to build moving forward.

Frequently, schools may adopt the state's definition for what it means for a student to be identified as gifted; however, they may also add to or modify that definition in order to fit the particular opportunities available to students. You might be surprised to know that there is not a single, agreed-upon definition of giftedness. In 1972, the Commissioner of Education, S. P. Marland Jr., assembled a report that was a landmark in establishing the basis for a definition of gifted. This report outlined six areas of giftedness: general intellectual ability, specific academic aptitude, creative or productive thinking, leadership ability, visual and performing arts, and psychomotor ability.
This idea of what gifted could encompass, as outlined in 1972, still drives many of the definitions seen in school systems today. In fact, researchers surveyed school districts and found that almost half utilized the

> DO YOU KNOW, SPECIFICALLY, HOW YOUR SCHOOL DEFINES GIFTED?

findings from Marland's report in structuring their gifted services (Plucker & Callahan, 2014). More recent work by Subotnik, Olszewski-Kubilius, and Worrell (2011) includes a definition of giftedness that acknowledges the domain-specific nature of giftedness, that psychosocial variables are an integral part of talent development, and that abilities "matter and need to be cultivated" (p. 7). You may notice similar language in your school's idea of what gifted is, or you may use this information in working to develop a functional definition for your purposes.

THEORIES OF GIFTEDNESS

Once you familiarize yourself with how your school defines giftedness, the next step is understanding the theory that drives instruction. If, in your search to find a definition of giftedness and its place in your school, you find an accompanying set of goals for gifted education, these goals are hopefully rooted in one or more of the theories discussed in this text. As you learn more about the history and nature of gifted education, come back to the theories discussed in this chapter and see if you notice some of the tenets playing out in the way your school identifies, serves, and supports its gifted students. Discussing educational theories might seem like a 5,000-foot aerial view approach, but I assure you that a basic understanding of what makes gifted education tick, so to speak, will be helpful as you move forward in designing learning for students, advocating for the program, and leading gifted education on your campus.

There are many prevailing theories about gifted education. The National Association for Gifted Children (NAGC, n.d.-b) outlined four major ones: Gagné's (1985) Differentiated Model of Giftedness and Talent (DMGT), Renzulli's (1978) Three-Ring Conception of Giftedness, Sternberg's (1999) Theory of Successful Intelligence, and Gardner's (1983) Theory of Multiple Intelligences. Although this is certainly not an exhaustive list of theories of gifted education, they are some of the most widely cited (Page, 2006; Plucker & Barab, 2005; Subotnik et al., 2011). This section explores the big ideas behind these theories in order to develop a better understanding of gifted education practices in your school.

Gagné's (1985) DMGT proposes a continuum of processes that work together to develop natural, untrained abilities (i.e., gifts) into talents (see Figure 1). According to Gagné, approximately 10% of students demonstrating natural ability and cultivated talents fit the "gifted" label. In this model, the role of chance interacts with environmental and interpersonal catalysts, coupled with natural physical or mental abilities, to influence the

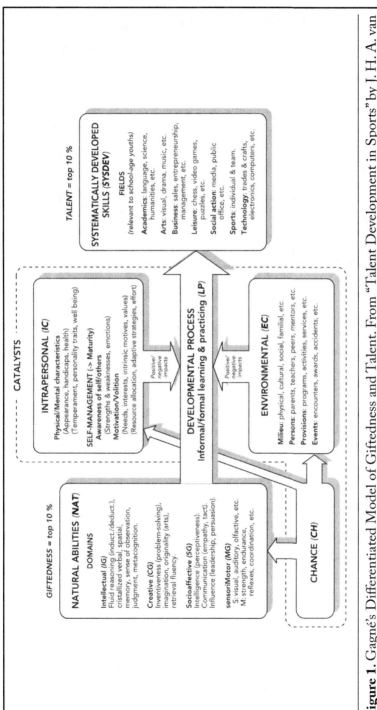

Figure 1. Gagné's Differentiated Model of Giftedness and Talent. From "Talent Development in Sports" by J. H. A. van Rossum and F. Gagné, in *The Handbook of Secondary Gifted Education* (p. 283), by F. A. Dixon and S. M. Moon (Eds.), 2006, New York, NY: Routledge Copyright 2006 by Taylor & Francis.

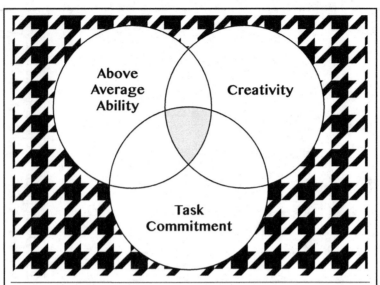

Figure 2. Three-Ring Conception of Giftedness. From *The Schoolwide Enrichment Model: A How-to Guide for Talent Development* (3rd ed., p. 22), by J. S. Renzulli and S. M. Reis, 2014, New York, NY: Routledge Copyright 2014 by Taylor & Francis. Reprinted with permission.

developmental process and develop talents. Gagné referred to these talents as "competencies," and they are developed in a variety of domain-specific areas.

Renzulli's (1978) Three-Ring Conception of Giftedness (see Figure 2) supports the idea that gifted behaviors interact with ability to manifest original, creative ideas and products. In this model, Renzulli departed from the notion of "schoolhouse giftedness," or the traditional type of academic achievement that many people believe to be synonymous with what it means to be gifted. Instead, the Three-Ring model focuses on developing creative-productive giftedness. This type of learning and productivity leverages specific academic strengths to create original products and ideas for authentic audiences. Like Gagné's (1985) DMGT, the goal of gifted education is to develop talents. Although both Renzulli and Gagné's models include elements of motivation, Renzulli's model relies heavily on students' achievement-oriented "gifted" behaviors.

Sternberg's (1999) Theory of Successful Intelligence seeks to build the skills needed to achieve success according to both one's personal standards and within a specific sociocultural context. Analytical, creative, and practical abilities are cultivated through learning how to adapt to, shape, and select environments in which a learner will be most successful. In this model, gifted learners plan, monitor, and evaluate goals and outcomes throughout a problem-solving process. Performance components of the Theory of Successful Intelligence include comparison and justification. Knowledge acquisition components include simply building one's knowledge to engage in problem solving. Like Gagné's (1985) DMGT, the role of environment is important in accounting for how talent is developed. Like Renzulli's (1978) Three-Ring Conception of Giftedness, Sternberg's model posits that to develop talent, students must be motivated to continue working toward the goal of producing or demonstrating advanced competencies, products, or skills.

The final model to discuss is Gardner's (1983) Theory of Multiple Intelligences. Gardner asserted that intelligence is manifested in many different domains in a variety of ways. He identified seven original intelligences: linguistic, logical-mathematical, visual-spatial, musical, bodily-kinesthetic, interpersonal, and intrapersonal. Later, in 1993, he added naturalistic intelligence to the list as well. Like the other three theorists, Gardner believed that an area of giftedness may stem from an innate talent or ability that then follows a developmental trajectory. Note that this theory, due to its lack of empirical backing, has fallen out of practice in many schools. I am discussing it here simply to build awareness and as

> **THE GOAL OF GIFTED SERVICES SHOULD BE TO DEVELOP ADVANCED TALENT IN STUDENTS WHO DEMONSTRATE THE ABILITY TO PERFORM AT EXCEPTIONAL LEVELS.**

a reminder to approach the idea of what giftedness is with a flexible and open mind. An important goal in all four of these theories is that gifted services should develop advanced talent in students who demonstrate the ability to perform at exceptional levels.

Your school may not subscribe to a singular theory of gifted education. Your school may have set goals for gifted education loosely based in one or more of these theories or specific district priorities. Regardless of whether there is direct alignment with these theories in your school's ideas about gifted programming, your understanding of what frames many gifted education practices today provides you with insight into the "why" of gifted education. In building your theoretical knowledge and understanding the definition and proposed goals of gifted education, you can construct a solid foundation and conceptual framework of the "what" and the "why." Identifying and understanding what defines giftedness in the context of your school, and how theory does or can drive practice, is the best first step in getting a hold on how your program and services work. If the resources outlining gifted services and programming at your school are slim, understanding and analyzing them is an important first step in establishing a solid base from which you can begin building learning opportunities for your students. In the case that you are starting from scratch, beginning with a clear vision and basic knowledge of theory will help to create a stable foundation.

BUILDING UP

With a clearer vision of the "what" by defining the term *gifted* and the "why" behind the services in place in your school, you can begin to think about decisions regarding curriculum and instruction. This next step in approaching such a vital component of gifted education puts the bricks on our metaphorical house.

Perhaps the closest you've come to working with gifted students was creating differentiated assignments for the kids in your general education classroom. The gifted teacher must discern what strategies and materials best meet student needs, interpret what constitutes meaningful curriculum versus "flash and trash," and identify resources that fit the structure of your services. This is a new experience for many teachers working in the gifted classroom for the first time. Begin by taking stock of what is available. Perhaps you have been left a collection of various lesson plans and resources from previous teachers. Your administration, parents, and students may be expecting the same kinds of activities or pet projects that previous teachers did with students, and you must decide whether or not to continue doing the same things. Or maybe you have been allocated a budget for the purchase of new instructional materials. Making sense of what is available, sorting through potential resources, and determining how to craft unique and responsive gifted services is a big task. Choosing which "bricks" to use to build effective content for your classroom should start with understanding what your students know and how gifted students learn.

DATA MATTER

Start by examining the identification criteria for gifted services in your school, as well as the data available for your students. What assessments and criteria does your school use to identify students for gifted services? Whatever curriculum you pursue should first line up with how students are identified, so that student services go on to support accurate and appropriate areas for talent development. For example, if your school utilizes academic achievement or ability scores as a metric for gifted assessment, look more closely into which specific academic areas students are tested. If the tests primarily assess reading and math, implementing curriculum that is heavily focused on creativity or leadership may not be appropriate. Both of those areas are worth exploring with students, but neither creativity nor leadership were examined when students were assessed for gifted services. Although some talents could be developed as a byproduct of implementing such curricula, those resources would not align directly with student needs.

A mismatch between the tests you give to identify students and the subsequent services you provide will not necessarily develop talent in the same way that tightly aligned identification and curriculum offerings will. Although Chapter 3 discusses identification and assessment in greater detail, note that your building blocks for learning and talent development (i.e., curriculum) should directly align to the evidence of advanced ability that placed your students in gifted services in the first place.

Getting a current snapshot of your students' needs through data that are already available is also necessary. For instance, do you have students who are in clear need of mathematical acceleration, based on their standardized assessment data, benchmarks, and grades? Are there students who are engaged in every science, technology, engineering, and math (STEM) elective, participate in all science-related extracurricular activities, and always seem to be in the labs? Do you have a cohort of talented writers or historians, whose test scores, writing portfolios, and classroom engagement (or lack thereof, which we will discuss in Chapter 5) evidence the need for advanced instruction? Tune in to the available data to answer these questions. Although your vested educational interest in these students should allow you to access specific academic information, if some data are unavailable you can always ask teachers. You can also use a student interest inventory at the beginning of the year, which can provide helpful data in terms of identifying specific areas for learning that will hook your students. Meeting current needs through high-interest content will help make sure your students are invested in learning from the get-go.

> **MEETING CURRENT NEEDS THROUGH HIGH-INTEREST CONTENT WILL HELP MAKE SURE YOUR STUDENTS ARE INVESTED IN LEARNING FROM THE GET-GO.**

WHAT MAKES CURRICULUM EFFECTIVE FOR GIFTED LEARNERS?

Gifted students need an aligned curriculum that uses principles of depth and complexity, authentic problem solving, and appropriate acceleration opportunities (VanTassel-Baska, 2015). Hockett (2009) analyzed five principles of high-quality curriculum that meet the needs of gifted learners. These principles are as follows:

- Principle 1: Curriculum utilizes big ideas or concepts to organize and explore discipline-based and integrative content.
- Principle 2: Curriculum explores content through abstraction, depth, breadth, and complexity.
- Principle 3: Curriculum engages students in thinking like disciplinarians. Highly effective curriculum for gifted students asks students to use processes and materials that allow them to interact with the content like a professional in the field.
- Principle 4: Curriculum emphasizes authentic, real-world problems, products, and performances. Outcomes of these experiences transform students' understanding and broaden their schemas.
- Principle 5: Curriculum is flexible in pacing and variety, and structured so that students can engage in self-directed learning and the pursuit of individual interests.

As a new gifted teacher, if you struggle with determining which curriculum resources to use or how to develop content, utilize these principles to support decisions that are best for your students' learning needs. These principles underscore the idea that curriculum does not necessarily have to come prescribed or in a kit with all of the instruction and supplies planned out for you. Although there are many quality gifted curricula that have detailed lesson plans and supply kits, if these materials do not allow for authentic problem solving or flexible pacing, then look at different options that are more adaptable. If the curriculum does not seem to introduce advanced, complex content and simply presents grade-level material in a "dressed up" way, then consider something else that better meets Principle 2. If you have been handed a set of resources or lesson plans that do not fit these principles, understand that it is okay to change or completely scrap the materials. As a new gifted teacher, you might be tempted to buy a one-and-done kit or just recycle the previous teacher's materials. However, if these resources do not fit with the principles outlined in this section, consider the possible outcomes: diminished creative productivity, missed opportunities for talent development, and disengagement with the material.

Although you do not need to reinvent the wheel, so to speak, having the confidence and knowledge to select new resources or modify existing ones is important when working with curriculum. That confidence is hard to come by, however, if you are responsible for teaching content that is new or with which you are uncomfortable. When I began teaching gifted, I shied away from math-related topics. I was a language arts teacher! What if the kids knew more than me about math and I could not teach them? (Let's be real . . . they definitely knew more than me.) What I failed to see was that although my role was to facilitate and guide learning, I could have sought out resources and strategies that encouraged student exploration and inquiry rather than put the burden of responsibility solely on my shoulders. Instead, I avoided teaching math deeply and reserved math activities as quick one-offs. Had I used the principles outlined, my curriculum selection and development would have placed the students at the center of learning, instead of me at the center of teaching. Understanding how gifted students best learn specific content areas, too, allows us insight into the types of learning opportunities and structures that put them squarely in the center of instruction. This section looks more deeply at the specific curricular needs of gifted learners in the four core academic subject areas. Coupling this information with the principles will certainly support your work in selecting and designing curriculum.

READING AND LANGUAGE ARTS

VanTassel-Baska (2017) established effective, straightforward criteria for selecting texts for gifted learners. First, texts for gifted readers must be at an appropriately advanced reading level, and contain rich vocabulary and sophisticated linguistic constructs. If you are working with student populations who are linguistically diverse, make sure the curriculum has appropriate scaffolds, such as models and organizers (Stambaugh, 2010) that help students articulate their written and verbal ideas. Appropriate texts for gifted learners should also be thematic in nature. Thematically linked readings will allow students to discuss both the big ideas within and across texts, as well as analyze literary devices that exemplify the author's craft (VanTassel-Baska, 2017). Texts should also be relevant to your student population; that is, they should reflect connections to your students' real worlds (Stambaugh, 2010) and allow gifted readers to connect with protagonists that share similar socioemotional traits (VanTassel-Baska, 2017). Including texts from diverse authors will also help to widen the scope of conversation around the text and expose students to a variety of perspectives.

The key to reading and language arts curriculum is to provide students with material that engages relevant topics through models of highly effective writing, which allows for discussion and written reflection that evidences a masterful understanding of the content. Students who interact with complex texts through reading, writing, and discussion grow their schemas and become effective analysts and authors who effectively connect themes, ideas, and meanings.

MATH

When selecting strategies and resources for teaching mathematics to advanced learners, remember Principle 3, that students should be encouraged to think like disciplinarians (Hockett, 2009). Research by Sriraman (2004) indicates that students gifted in math think differently, and their thinking resembles that of professional mathematicians. Curriculum that focuses on big mathematical concepts (Gavin, Casa, Adelson, Carroll, & Sheffield

2009) and challenges students to inquire, problem solve, and discuss (VanTassel-Baska, 2003) like professionals will engage and grow mathematically gifted students. Gavin et al. (2009) warned against assembling piecemeal activities and work that is slightly above grade level to act as the primary curriculum in the gifted math classroom. Concepts, skills, and abstractions should have a meaningful flow and build on one another. Students should understand how the content that they are learning is situated in the real world. Although there is nothing wrong with allowing students to move on to more challenging, accelerated work when they have demonstrated mastery on mathematical concepts or providing substitution activities that engage students at a higher level, these should not be the primary means of advanced math instruction. Material that teaches skills in isolation or requires lots of rote memorization may not be best suited to advanced learners. Activities that require students to practice rigorous mathematical thinking and engage them like professionals in the field are earmarks of effective gifted math curriculum. Content and structure should allow for flexible pacing, because even in a gifted classroom you may have some students who need additional time and support in mastering concepts.

> STUDENTS SHOULD UNDERSTAND HOW THE CONTENT THAT THEY ARE LEARNING IS SITUATED IN THE REAL WORLD.

When evaluating math resources, look for opportunities to solve authentic problems, determine the appropriateness of certain strategies in realistic situations, and find connections between their mathematical learning and environment. Although this is certainly good for all students, allowing mathematically gifted kids to engage with advanced content at a pace that keeps up with their ability, all while encouraging them to think like mathematicians, will most successfully develop mathematical talent.

SOCIAL STUDIES

Little, Feng, VanTassel-Baska, Rogers, and Avery (2007) analyzed gifted social studies curricula and identified several key traits of effective curriculum for gifted students:

- the framework for the curriculum was built around critical thinking, historical analysis, and interpreting primary sources;
- the interdisciplinary concept of "systems" was the focus of the learning; and
- although historical analysis and text interpretation were the focus of the curriculum, the material facilitated opportunities to make important interdisciplinary connections and supported an inquiry-based approach to learning.

Social studies topics lend themselves very well to interdisciplinary learning and provide students many opportunities to make abstract connections within and across disciplines. With such a wide scope of possibility, you must examine not only the quality of the material used, but also the strategies employed for learning. Activities should center around best-practice learning strategies, such as concept mapping and metacognition, and reiterate research skills, and lesson outcomes should align with the goals of the overall curricular framework ("Selecting Curricula," 2004). Social studies curriculum may employ scenario-based opportunities to apply major concepts and give students a chance to act as politicians, historians, and geographers in order to make the content real and engaging. When students can use their learning to make decisions and test different outcomes in an inquiry or scenario-based setting, they are using their knowledge and skills far more critically than simply understanding. Curriculum that uses big ideas to guide learning make connections between figures, people, and events—not necessarily in a strict timeline structure— and engages gifted learners in ways that challenge them to look for trends across places and time.

You may also consider integrating social studies extensions into areas like science or language arts so that the learning is situated in real-life problems, or serves to illustrate the historical significance of the content. Social studies concepts are found across disciplines, and encouraging your students to think like historians in all subject areas helps to situate learning, and also presents additional opportunities to make meaningful, authentic connections.

science

Principal 3, thinking like a disciplinarian (Hockett, 2009), is a critical component of science curriculum for gifted learners. In order to develop science talent, curriculum must provide students with opportunities to engage in and internalize scientific process, such as observation, experimentation, and measurement—all in the context of behaving like a scientist in the field (Chandler, 2012). Chandler emphasized the importance of adopting an "attitudinal mindset that views the world through the lens of a scientist" (p. 113) and that can be fostered through hands-on investigation, collaborating with real experts in the field, and ample opportunity to engage in the inquiry process. VanTassel-Baska (1998) reiterated the need to focus on inquiry through problem-based learning and including meaningful technology application.

CHOOSING AND IMPLEMENTING QUALITY CURRICULUM IN THE GIFTED CLASSROOM IS A RECURSIVE PROCESS THAT IS NEVER REALLY FINISHED.

Gifted science curriculum is not a set of isolated experiments or lab activities. These hands-on pieces should highlight and underscore the experimental design process thinking that happens as students identify authentic problems and focus on big learning concepts. Effective curriculum engages diverse strategies that help students make abstract connections and generate original solutions (VanTassel-Baska, 1998, 2003). Students should be posing and answering overarching questions, and using the inquiry process to seek information, build knowledge, and problem solve like scientists in the field.

When reviewing or developing gifted science curriculum, finding a series of hands-on activities that are fun and student led is easy, but these activites may lack context or real-world applicability. Context and real-wold applicability should be the outcome goals, with an emphasis on creative production to solve problems. Gifted science curriculum should feature lots of student-led activities, but remember that the activities and learning strategies employed should tie back directly to the overall goals and objectives of the curriculum.

PUTTING IT ALL TOGETHER

Understanding how to put together the "what," "why," and "how" behind gifted education helps you establish a solid foundation from which you can plan challenging, appropriate, highly effective instruction for gifted learners. You have your most important building materials ready to go. But just like building a house, unexpected things happen and you have to be ready to refigure, rescale, and rework. Choosing and implementing quality curriculum in the gifted classroom is a recursive process that is never really finished.

The goal of this chapter is to establish a clear understanding of who your gifted students are, how they are served, and what are some of the best practices for meeting their academic needs. Moving forward, check back on your foundation and use it to guide decision making. Not only does foundational awareness provide a cohesive learning experience for your students, but it also helps you track what works and what doesn't, aids in tying together practice, purposes, and products, and sets a clear roadmap that allows you to reflect, and plan your route ahead effectively.

CHAPTER 2
HOW DO GIFTED SERVICES "FIT IN"?

Equipped with an understanding of what giftedness means and how you can facilitate authentic, effective learning opportunities for these students, the next step in building a strong program is examining how gifted services fit into the overall structure of your school. Does your school focus on differentiation in the general education classroom to meet the needs of gifted students? Do gifted services provide students with enrichment activities not available in general education or elective classes? Is the role of gifted programming to develop talent parallel to general education classes through enrichment and extension? Is your school's program structured to provide accelerated content? Are there different types of services to students at varying tiers or levels? There are so many questions that lead to the exploration of many different possibilities in terms of ways in which programs and services can be structured. Identifying the specific ways in which student needs are met in your school and how meeting those needs fits into the overall structure of your school is the next big step in understanding and evaluating (or building) your current program. Gifted identification, service design, and curriculum must support one another and function as a cohesive unit that serves to develop student talents. If the theory of gifted students' defining traits and educational needs is the foundation and building blocks for learning and talent development, then the service design provides the framework.

If you are new to the field of gifted education, you may not be aware of all of the possible structures for service design. This chapter will focus on some of the most common. You may find that your school's program has room for growth. You may discover that there are possibilities for working with gifted students of which you were previously unaware, and this could create a whole new set of choices you can use to build out your program. This chapter will outline four models of gifted education. Although these structures are fairly typical, they are not the only ways to provide services to students. Many schools take innovative and creative approaches to gifted service design, so please keep in mind that it never hurts to think outside of the box.

Before discussing the models in depth, knowing the underlying tenets of what makes an effective programmatic structure is important. Rogers (2007) outlined a set of lessons learned from the study of many different types of gifted programs:

- Criterion 1: Gifted learners need daily challenges in their specific areas of identified academic need.
- Criterion 2: Gifted learners should have regular opportunities to be unique and work independently in their areas of interest.
- Criterion 3: Provisions for various forms of acceleration should be available to gifted learners, as their educational needs require.

Extending your learning into criteria for what makes an effective model for programming can help guide you as you work to develop your program. As you learn more about the models in this chapter, come back to these criteria and ask (a) if you think that you can reasonably meet the expectations within a selected model, and (b) if it best meets the needs of your students given their academic needs, as indicated through your identification measures and ongoing assessment.

FOUR MODELS OF GIFTED EDUCATION

DIFFERENTIATION

The most basic model for serving gifted students is to differentiate within a general education classroom. Educators have heard for decades about how important differentiating is for the varied needs of the students in their classrooms, and they understand how challenging differentiation can be. Tomlinson (2008) outlined major principles of differentiation, which include flexible and open approaches to content, varied pedagogical strategies or processes, and individualized student products that reflect the learners' expression, as well as the targeted skills or standards. When differentiation for gifted students occurs in a general education classroom, there should be a combination of interest and learning centers, areas for students to work individually, and opportunities to leverage instructional technology to support students in both learning and product-generating (Dinnocenti, 1998). Students in a differentiated classroom should be able to interact with learning standards at a cognitive level that is appropriately challenging—regardless of what that level may be. The teacher acts as a facilitator and is responsible for maintaining ongoing data and progress monitoring for students.

Anyone with teaching experience can tell you that in a large, heterogeneously grouped class, differentiation is hard to do well and consistently. Gifted learners are often overlooked within a differentiation model because teachers are (understandably) concerned with filling the gaps of and intervening with students who struggle to master grade-level standards. A class with one or two students identified as gifted may many times fall short in providing the time and appropriate materials for effective differentiation. Schools relying on this model to provide regular, appropriate services to their gifted learners can combat this issue in a couple of different ways. Gifted students can be cluster grouped, a practice that assigns gifted students into the same class section so that there is a cluster of advanced students in a class. A larger cohort of advanced learners allows the students flexibility to work with like-ability peers and helps the teacher put gifted instruction at the forefront of planning because there is a significant percentage of gifted students in the classroom who need similar levels of complexity and/or accelerated content.

You may be the teacher who is assigned a gifted cluster-grouped class, and expectations for differentiation are that you provide opportunities for students to master content at a quicker pace (i.e., compacting) so that they may engage in more deep and complex ways with the material. In a differentiation model, you should preassess before instruction so that, based on student levels of mastery, you're able to provide vocabulary at a higher Lexile, engage in less repetition, teach processes and systems that are advanced, take more time in hands-on investigations, and interact with complex learning material. Gifted students in a differentiated classroom may be learning the same standards as their grade-level peers (i.e., the what), but the pace and ways in which students demonstrate mastery (the how) should be commensurate with their advanced levels of skill and comprehension.

> **STUDENTS IN A DIFFERENTIATED CLASSROOM SHOULD BE ABLE TO INTERACT WITH LEARNING STANDARDS AT A COGNITIVE LEVEL THAT IS APPROPRIATELY CHALLENGING—REGARDLESS OF WHAT THAT LEVEL MAY BE.**

Your role as a gifted teacher may be to support general education teachers in providing meaningful differentiation. You can do this through collaborating and planning for coteach or push-in opportunities with the classroom teacher. As a second teacher in the classroom, you may pull the cluster-grouped gifted students to work on an extension of the general education curriculum. In a math class, this could take the form of piggybacking on the standards and working at an accelerated pace so that students gain exposure to concepts and skills that are above grade level. In reading, language arts, and social studies, this could mean reading and writing about advanced text sets that enrich and extend the classroom content and providing opportunities for higher level discourse and analysis. A small group of gifted students in science might move on to above-grade-level concepts and follow through with more complex hands-on investigations. A coteach model that includes a gifted education teacher has the potential to provide regular, effective differentiation that meets the needs of gifted students.

If your time as a gifted teacher is more limited to periodic push-ins, strategic planning with the general education teacher for advanced learning experiences is essential. Carving out time to work with the teacher to identify key standards or skills will help you create engaging experiences for students in the classroom. If you do not have the time for daily teaching opportunities, you may consider planning opportunities for introducing advanced content from which students can begin working independently. Your work as a push-in teacher may be to help students design and work through independent projects that they would then be able to attend to daily in the classroom, and you would provide regularly scheduled support. Or you may push in to the classroom with an advanced center or workshop rotation planned, and spend time working on this with gifted students through a workshop format. If your role focuses more on helping the teacher to plan for gifted differentiation, you can always provide opportunities to periodically coteach, launch a new unit, and meet with students in addition to supporting the teacher through planning.

Remember that if your primary role is to support differentiation, time is of the essence. Advocate for built-in planning time in your schedule so that you can focus on identifying and creating meaningful, challenging resources to share with teachers and students. Without this time, collaboration with other teachers will be surface level, at best, and pockets of sporadic time in which you do plan will not make for high-quality differentiation practices. In advocating for protected time, keep consistent services, academically appropriate learning opportunities, and high student outcomes at the forefront of these conversations. Yes, your students have above-average abilities; however, they need regular, appropriate challenge to maximize achievement and develop talent. They can only get that through your hard work, planning, and collaboration with other teachers. Being a vocal advocate for protected time helps to ensure quality differentiation resources to make sure gifted services consistently benefit the students who need them.

Differentiation is the most basic model for meeting the needs of gifted students. The investment in time and purposeful planning to develop preassessment strategies, extensions, and opportunities for content acceleration pays off when students are able to develop talent and skills every day. Whether you are the teacher providing this service or you support a differentiated classroom through push-in, coteaching, or planning, remember that this model is intended to challenge gifted students daily, with academically-appropriate opportunities to learn.

PARALLEL CURRICULUM MODEL

In this model of gifted education, based on the work of Tomlinson et al. (2009), qualitatively differentiated curriculum is designed to support the abilities, interests, and learning preferences of individual students. This model focuses on the unique needs of each learner and aims to support learning through four different curricular areas: the core curriculum, the curriculum of connections, the curriculum of practice, and the curriculum of identity.

The core curriculum involves the big ideas underlying the learning. These may be principles, skills, or understandings that provide the foundation for what students will be able to know, understand, and do. The curriculum of connections, or the inter- or crossdisciplinary connections associated with the core curriculum, has an organic quality to it in that the teacher may design lessons that exemplify and explore specific connections, but students may also connect the core curriculum to ideas that are unique to their schemas. Allowing students to explore the types of meaning that they can make within and across the content is essential to supporting a robust curriculum of connections. The curriculum of practice is the "doing" part of learning. Here, students can apply their learning in a variety of settings. As with all practice, students may find that they need to reimagine, retweak, and rework their ideas and strategies several times until they master the curriculum of doing. Finally, the curriculum of identity includes student reflection on their learning, how it has supported the growth in their interests, knowledge, disciplinary skills, as well as ways in which their learning might have applications in the future. In all of these curricular focus areas, learning is product-oriented, which means that students will interact with the material in a way that facilitates an abstract or concrete end product (Tomlinson et al., 2009).

Through a variety of experiences that utilize concepts of differentiation, extension, and enrichment, teachers create curriculum that is adaptive to the unique needs and interests of gifted learners. The curriculum is "parallel" not because all of the four curricula are happening at once; rather, the four types of curricula are ways in which a teacher can approach curriculum design (Tomlinson et al., 2007). The teacher is the expert and can use his or her knowledge of both the content and the students to design curriculum that allows for students to interact with the material in a variety of different ways. The Parallel Curriculum Model acts as a guide, not a formula, for creating curriculum.

ALLOWING STUDENTS TO EXPLORE THE TYPES OF MEANING THAT THEY CAN MAKE WITHIN AND ACROSS THE CONTENT IS ESSENTIAL TO SUPPORTING A ROBUST CURRICULUM OF CONNECTIONS.

Your school may have a designated pull-out or gifted class time when students participate in the types of learning experiences outlined in the Parallel Curriculum Model. Enrichment programs like these typically focus on higher level thinking and processing skills, creativity, self-selected projects, and authentic, in-depth exploration of a real-world topic or problem (Kim, 2016). Many times, this is a differentiated service model for gifted students that offers content not otherwise addressed in general education or elective courses.

If you are charged with providing services through this structure, you may be overwhelmed with ideas about how to start or where to go. Done well, enrichment through a varied approach to curriculum has been proven to have positive impacts on both gifted students' academic achievement and socioemotional development (Kim, 2016). But how can you be sure you're providing effective learning opportunities that appropriately support your students in developing their talents? Let's go back to the criteria: How will you ensure that students get challenged daily, particularly if your enrichment class is only once or a few times per week? How will you provide your students the opportunity for individual study? How can you build in structures for acceleration? Recall Hockett's (2009) principles outlined in Chapter 1. They tell you that utilizing big ideas or concepts to organize and explore content; emphasizing authentic, real-world problems, products, and performances; and flexibly pacing and organizing content so that students can engage in self-directed learning are what define curriculum for gifted learners. Go back to these principles as you consider ways to structure the learning content within the Parallel Curriculum Model.

You may consider organizing lessons around big ideas, themes, or archetypes based on your students' interests. With interest inventories or strategic planned experiences (i.e., Socratic seminars, problem-based inquiry), you can identify overarching topics that are relevant and engaging to students. Once topics have been identified, you can select one that has the potential to make connections to the areas in which your students have been identified for giftedness. For example, if your students are interested in space exploration and identified for giftedness in math, there are many ways to orient mathematical learning toward space concepts. The selected topic should have both concrete and abstract crosscurricular connections that you can tie back to your students' identified areas for talent development.

Once a topic has been selected, you can link these abstract concepts to real-world connections and encourage students to explore the topic in your class through discussion, hands-on exploration, and project-based learning. Understanding complex ideas may be accomplished through teaching content that is above grade level, which allows for students to experience an appropriate academic challenge. Providing extensions for students to study facets of the topic, or tangentially related subjects that are of interest to individual students through independent learning contracts, gives students access to opportunities for daily interaction with advanced, individualized learning. Implemented thoughtfully and with purpose, this approach to gifted education curriculum has the potential to add a new dimension to students' overall academic experience.

As the teacher utilizing this approach to instruction, you will continual add resources and ideas to your collection. Your students will change and so will their interests. As you plan day-to-day, semester-to-semester, and year-to-year, remember that the learning plan must not only meet the criteria for an effective program model, but also take into account the very real constraints of time, money, and space. Many times, teachers fall into the trap of thinking that content has to culminate in a big project of some kind; this may not be reasonable if you see the students for 30 minutes per week in another teacher's classroom. Additionally, if your strategies and topics change to adapt to a new cohort of students, amassing lots of specific resources is not practical. Gifted programs should provide students with the opportunity to advance their knowledge and develop their talents through exposure to complex ideas, and this does not always mean a big showy product at the end. This might not be reasonable or appropriate. Remember, the product orientation of the Parallel Curriculum Model includes both concrete and abstract products. Abstract products include transferable learning outcomes, problem-solving strategies, attitudes, beliefs, and personal and social development (Tomlinson et al., 2009). The rigor in the gifted classroom should be found in the academic learning and development that takes place in students, not just the final product. Just because a product is big and flashy does not mean it is rigorous or challenging. Effective curriculum facilitates growth through complex, in-depth products or ideas that grow students' understandings, skills, and talents. The Parallel Curriculum Model provides teachers with a variety of ways to approach content development that is conducive to developing student talent through a variety of opportunities for advanced, interest-based learning.

INTEGRATED CURRICULUM MODEL

Whereas the Parallel Curriculum Model focuses on approaching learning through curriculum that enriches and extends student understanding, VanTassel-Baska's (2003) Integrated Curriculum Model (ICM) is a three-dimensional model that leverages both in-depth exploration of content and acceleration. The ICM features an advanced content dimension and supports acceleration practices so that students can move rapidly through advanced content (VanTassel-Baska & Brown, 2007). "Rapidly" means at a pace that is conducive to student learning; once students have demonstrated mastery of a concept, they may move on to material that is advanced. This advancement should continue until students are learning in their appropriate zone of proximal development (ZPD), regardless of the grade level of that content (Stanley, 1993). The model's process-product dimension encourages in-depth, independent learning by incorporating higher order thinking and processing (VanTassel-Baska & Brown, 2007). In this dimension, students have opportunities to interact with information at complex levels through reasoning processes that might be specific to a task or generalizable to a variety of situations (i.e., divergent thinking strategies or the engineering design process). The thematic dimension focuses students' learning on major issues, themes, and ideas with theoretical and real-world applications (VanTassel-Baska & Wood, 2010). In this model of gifted education, third-grade students may be discussing ways in which mathematical and physics concepts could be utilized to solve a real-world problem, or fifth-grade students may be reading and analyzing thematically-linked pieces of literature that are well beyond their grade level standards or expected Lexile levels. The ICM strives to create a match between the ZPD of the learner, the pace of instruction, and content of the material.

What does the advanced content dimension mean for a teacher using the ICM? It means that you may have several students working on various levels of content, processes, and products in the same classroom. One implication is that teachers who are effective in this model select resources that span beyond the scope of one grade level and are willing to collaborate with teachers of different grade levels to appropriately scaffold content. These teachers are willing to allow students to learn at their own pace and help students to master content so that they can move on to something more advanced. Another implication is that teachers need to rethink the way in which they evaluate students' learning. Rather than requiring students to ace a prescribed milestone in order to move on to more advanced content, teachers continually engage students in feedback on their learning and understandings, and evaluate readiness for advancement based on performance or demonstrated competency. An approach to evaluation that looks more like mastery learning than traditional grading helps teachers understand not only exactly where students are in their learning, but also when moving on to the next learning target is appropriate. Employing a mastery-

> THE MOST WORTHWHILE LEARNING IS THE KIND THAT WILL DEVELOP YOUR STUDENTS' CAPACITY TO ANALYZE, EVALUATE, AND CREATE IN A VARIETY OF CONTEXTS, NOT JUST ON A PARTICULAR TASK.

oriented view of how learning is paced also has positive effects on student attitude toward content and instruction and could result in more effective time and attention spent on task (Kulik, Kulik, & Bangert-Drowns, 1990).

Teachers engaging students in the process-product dimension advance student knowledge, skills, and understandings by supporting ways in which students can think about and interact with the content. If a task or an idea requires a specific type of approach, such as the experimental design process mentioned in a previous chapter, teachers engage students as disciplinarians to recursively think about and solve problems using certain strategies or approaches. If the task is more open-ended or ill-defined, students may use a variety of synthesis, evaluation, and problem-solving techniques. Teachers can promote the types of thinking that lead to advanced processes and products through facilitating activities that encourage ideational fluency, evaluation of ideas, foreseeing implications, chaining problem elements, spontaneous flexibility (Rosenfield & Houtz, 1978), analyzing ill-defined problems (Welter, Jaarsveld, & Lachmann, 2018), and presenting situations in which quantitative and verbal reasoning are applied in novel settings or ways. When designing learning opportunities for students, remember that the thinking is a means to an end, rather than the end itself. Many curriculum resources tout the ability to build creative thinking skills, similar to the ones listed here, and promise creative student products. As you examine these resources, remember that the most worthwhile learning is the kind that will develop your students' capacity to analyze, evaluate, and create in a variety of contexts, not just on a particular task. The process-product dimension seeks to build students' creative productivity and challenge their thinking in both situation-specific and general scenarios.

Learning in the thematic dimension is centered on big ideas, issues, or themes that connect to real-world concepts. Perhaps this takes the form of essential questions to solve an authentic problem, or a thematic approach to understanding a collection of ideas. The goal of organizing the learning into important aspects of a discipline, understood in a systematic way, is to ensure a deep understanding of the discipline rather than a collection of facts that embody a topic (VanTassel-Baska & Wood, 2010). Students who are charged to think like authors, scientists, and mathematicians will be able to synthesize knowledge and apply it in a way that could solve a real-life problem. This is where the three dimensions converge. When students are allowed to access cognitively appropriate content, think about it in ways that stretch their creative problem-solving and productivity skills, and understand how their learning fits into a bigger picture, they will generate products and ideas at sophisticated levels, much like actual practitioners in the field. The teacher facilitates this by organizing content and material that follow patterns, invite students to problem find and problem solve in an authentic context, and purposefully tie back the learning to the theme, big idea, or issue. Curriculum that is flexible, scaffolded, and allows students to both deductively and inductively approach and solve problems best supports learning in the ICM.

Teachers utilizing the ICM to design their curriculum may run into some very real issues. Other teachers from higher grade levels may say, "You can't teach that in elementary—I teach that in middle school." If gifted instruction is in a pull-out or enrichment class, you may have other general education teachers asking, "What do students do when they're in my class and have already learned about that?" Responding appropriately to the questions and concerns of teachers will require openness and collaboration. Showing middle school teachers how students are interacting with the content as advanced elementary learners could give the teachers ideas about possible extension opportunities for their classrooms or open up a conversation about the ways in which they can piggyback on the content taught in the elementary gifted setting to allow students to advance even more at the middle school level. Also keep in mind that learning based on academic standards is cumulative and does not exist in a silo. Just as one would look at below-grade-level standards in order to understand where a student needing intervention may have formed a gap, one should also look at above-grade-level standards to determine how to meet the needs of the advanced learner. Otherwise, gifted students will not make the same academic gains from year to year as their grade-level peers. The depth and rigor of the content may change from grade to grade, but students cannot be restricted to a single year's worth of learning if their cognitive capabilities necessitate that they advance.

If students have already learned what a teacher plans to teach, then offer to form a partnership so that you can help that teacher create learning opportunities that extend the content, or identify areas in which students can work independently on advanced material while whole-group instruction focuses on the material that they have already mastered. As a gifted teacher, your role is to help others understand that students benefit from going at a pace that is appropriate for their developmental level, and if that level requires acceleration, then that is what is best for the students, period. A music teacher would not make a piano student play music from the same book until all of the other students in the classroom caught up. This would stifle the young musician's talent and hamper his or her development. The same is true for not allowing advanced students to accelerate in appropriate subject areas. Students accelerated in appropriate subject areas, or ones in which they have demonstrated mastery, show substantial, positive academic effects in those areas (Colangelo, Assouline, & Gross, 2004). This is really a win-win for both gifted students and their content-area teachers; you as a gifted teacher may need to help explain what this looks like in practical application and facilitate structures that support advanced student learning.

The ICM is responsive to student needs in terms of both high-interest content and pacing. It can be a great model to facilitate smooth transitions between the gifted and regular classrooms, and it has the potential to foster positive collaboration between you and other teachers. Planning for the what and the how of the ICM, just like you would for differentiation, is key in making sure students are able to interact with content and resources that yield advanced, high-quality products and ideas, demonstrative of ongoing talent development.

SCHOOLWIDE ENRICHMENT MODEL

Does your school's program provide different types of services to students at varying tiers? If so, you may be working in a structure that looks much like the Schoolwide Enrichment

Model (SEM; Renzulli & Reis, 2014). This model, which seeks to develop creativity and talent, engages all students through opportunities in the general education curriculum, as well as students identified for gifted services. The SEM begins by introducing all students to basic enrichment opportunities (i.e., guest speakers, special presentations, field trips, etc.). These are known as Type I experiences, and they lay the foundation for exploration in the next two tiers. Type II involves identifying students for a talent pool, frequently though the use of assessment data and proficiency on performance-based tasks maintained in a portfolio, as well as student interest. Students in the talent pool are eligible for additional enrichment experiences. These experiences engage creative problem-solving activities, the development of specific skill sets, and the use of advanced level material (Reis & Renzulli, 2009). Finally, students who express the motivation, commitment, and skill move into Type III. Here, students engage in self-selected research and the development of advanced, sophisticated products.

If this model forms the basis for your school's gifted services, there are several components to look at. First, how are all students given the opportunity to interact with enrichment material? Gifted teachers may facilitate planned experiences for all students in a classroom, or your school may have frequent opportunities for enrichment, such as author visits, career-related speakers, or in-school field trips. Creating these opportunities can be a collaborative partnership between school administration and general education teachers, as well as the gifted teacher. You can provide feedback about enrichment that helps to spark interest and is most useful in inspiring and motivating the types of creative productivity that occur in Types II and III.

The formation of a talent pool, particularly, may vary widely from school to school. Does your school rely primarily on assessment data, such as achievement and ability tests? If so, be cautioned that relying on quantitative data alone can preclude a number of students with potential from participating in Type II and III activities. Reis and Renzulli (2009) advocated for the use of portfolios in tandem with assessment data so that student creativity and task commitment can be exemplified, as these traits are important in success in subsequent tiers. Portfolios can take a variety of formats, and deciding how to structure and evaluate these pieces of qualitative data should be agreed upon by both the gifted teacher and campus administrative team. Providing students with every opportunity to demonstrate their readiness and ability to move into Type II activities will help to ensure that your talent pool is as inclusive as possible.

Once students are identified for the talent pool, the gifted teacher will work with the general education teacher to compact curriculum in order to create more time for students to engage in creative thinking activities that will lead to the development of unique products. These may be shorter-term projects, activities that extend the enrichment experiences from Type I, or exploratory activities based on student interest. Students working in Type II may spend time attending pull-out classes, and the gifted teacher may support these students in the general education classroom or may spend the bulk of his or her time planning with the classroom teacher on compacting and providing appropriate extension opportunities. Whatever the format Type II activities take, the gifted teacher should take an active role in providing the support and resources for students to deepen

> **A TIERED APPROACH TO GIFTED SERVICES REQUIRES THE GIFTED TEACHER TO BE TUNED IN TO STUDENT INTERESTS, PROFICIENT WITH ONGOING ASSESSMENT STRATEGIES, AND FLEXIBLE IN APPROACHES TO INSTRUCTION AND STUDENT SUPPORT.**

their interest and knowledge so that students have opportunities to be creative producers.

From the talent pool identified in Type II, some of these students will express the capability and desire to move into Type III activities. Although some students will be working at an appropriate challenge level in Type II, others will share ideas that can be accomplished through self-directed learning and the generation of an advanced product or performance. Remember, here, that determining who is suited to move into Type III activities should include both a quantitative and qualitative approach. Students who demonstrate mastery quickly in Type II, ask challenging questions, demonstrate appropriate self-direction and motivation, and benefit from a compacted and accelerated general education curriculum are good candidates for Type III enrichment. When evaluating how the tiers work in your school, ask questions such as, "How fluid is the movement between tiers?", "How much student choice is involved in movement between tiers?", and, "Do the products and processes generated in Tier III demonstrate high levels of creative productivity and talent development?"

As a gifted teacher working in a tiered service model, the key considerations at the forefront are certainly how ongoing assessment works, the ways in which you can partner with general education teachers to compact and accelerate the core curriculum, and how to provide ongoing support to those students as they engage in the creative-productive process. Gifted teachers working in a tiered service model may take on a variety of roles and responsibilities. Look for creative ways to engage students on all levels, and partner with teachers in order to maximize positive student impact through this model. A tiered approach to gifted services requires the gifted teacher to be tuned in to student interests, proficient with ongoing assessment strategies, and flexible in approaches to instruction and student support. If you are working in this service model, first and foremost establish clear expectations with your instructional leadership team, and then focus on understanding your student demographic so that you can plan appropriate Type I and II experiences. Familiarize yourself with the structure of assessment and movement between tiers, and identify areas in which you can most effectively support teachers and students.

Starting here gives you a clear direction and a sound foundation for later growing and expanding opportunities for students.

WHAT DO GIFTeD SeRVICeS LOOK LIKe In MY SCHOOL?

After having read through the four models of gifted education outlined in this chapter, you may recognize components from a few different models at work on your campus. Your school's gifted program may be in a transition or developmental phase, and you are seeking to grow and establish its future. Understanding the models discussed here will help you enhance your knowledge of the structures and possibilities for creating a program that meets the needs of your students, as well as the constraints of time, space, and resources in your school. Recognizing pieces from the ICM or tenets of differentiation may inspire you to modify or create programmatic opportunities for your students that have not previously been available. Whatever your level of involvement is in developing and contributing to your program's structure, being familiar with what different models look like will support you in brainstorming new possibilities for your students.

To get a bigger picture of how the different opportunities and services come together for gifted students in your school, utilizing the Unified Program Design model (Rubenstein & Ridgley, 2017) is very helpful. The Unified Program Design (see Figure 3) delineates the aspects defining gifted programs and illustrates how your existing model addresses the different components. In this model, the two main components of a gifted program are the delivery method and curriculum—these are the big ideas we have discussed thus far in Chapters 1 and 2. The framework of this model synthesizes these two components in order to demonstrate how all of the parts of the program work together.

As you use this model to visualize how your school's program comes together to support gifted learners, look at the various components. Does your program structure meet the criteria listed at the beginning of the chapter? Do the how (structure of services)

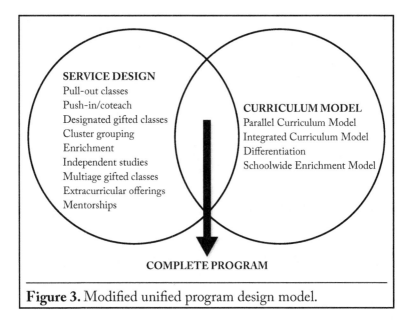

Figure 3. Modified unified program design model.

and the what (curriculum and additional student offerings) mirror your current assessment practices? Using the Unified Program Design model to get a 10,000-foot view of your program may help you to identify areas of need. You may find yourself reflecting and making realizations associated with identification and services. ("We identify students using a creativity measure, but there's not really an explicit curricular piece that addresses this.") You may notice areas that can be streamlined or need additional supports. ("We have two gifted service structures that address English language arts, but none for science.") You may also see places in which your program tightly aligns and successfully meets student needs, and use this as a best practice model moving forward. ("We have great opportunities for our gifted math students to have compacted instruction in the general education classroom, and G/T math provides accelerated content.")

If you are in the early stages of helping develop structures for gifted services, using the Unified Program Design model can also assist you in sketching out possibilities. This is a great model to facilitate conversations between stakeholders, as well as advocate for appropriate resources, when examining the various possibilities for gifted services. Having an illustration of exactly what gifted services encompass and accomplish is also useful when forming partnerships with general education teachers, so you can show them clearly how gifted and talented programs fit into the overall academic structure of the school. You can also use this visual to advocate for resources that will help meet specific academic, social, and developmental student needs in areas that fall short of achieving these goals. Remember the criteria outlined at the beginning of this chapter: Gifted learners need daily challenges in their specific areas of identified academic need; gifted learners should have regular opportunities to be unique and work independently in their areas of interest; and provisions for various forms of acceleration should be available to gifted learners, as their educational needs require (Rogers, 2007). Outlining the ways in which those criteria are met, or areas in which additional supports are needed, helps teachers and instructional leaders alike make informed, student-centered decisions about gifted programs and services.

CHAPTER 3

STUDENT IDENTIFICATION, SERVICES, AND SUPPORT

Teaching gifted students is not all aha moments, fun projects, and spending time with students who share your love of learning. You likely have additional responsibilities that include student assessment, as well as monitoring and intervention with individuals when needed. Students identified for gifted services are frequently not gifted in all subject areas, nor are they prepared at all times to work with advanced products and processes without scaffolding on the part of the teacher. These students may also struggle when challenged, have issues with motivation, and at times, require academic intervention. The gifted teacher fills a number of roles in addition to providing instruction, and has to be flexible and resourceful in order to help fulfill the responsibilities that come with working in a gifted and talented program.

Chapters 1 and 2 discussed the importance of coherence between student identification, appropriate curriculum selection, and service design. This chapter will talk more explicitly about the role of student identification and how gifted teachers can ensure that, once identified, these students have access to the most appropriate resources and structures for talent development. Understanding how you can meet the varied needs of your students will then help you best support and advocate for gifted students' ongoing growth and success.

IDENTIFICATION

The process of student identification can vary widely from district to district. Gifted advocacy organizations, such as NAGC, support the use of both objective (quantitative) and subjective (qualitative) measures, so that the identification process encompasses both performance and potential in a diverse body of learners. A critical point to remember when discussing student assessment and identification is that the identification and classification of high-ability and gifted individuals should reflect standards and goals of the program for which the assessment is being conducted (Pierson, Kilmer, Rothlisberg, & McIntosh 2012). This process of identification, according to NAGC (n.d.-b), "follow[s] a systematic, multi-phased process" that includes nomination or identification, screening or selection, and placement into gifted services.

You likely recognize these structures in your gifted program. Students may be nominated, or referred, for gifted screening by teachers, parents, other professionals (such as a tutor or counselor), or themselves. Some schools identify students through designated assessments, while others may use a system of observations and planned experiences orchestrated by the gifted department, while others positively identify students through existing test scores. Additional data, such as teacher and parent feedback, as well as work samples, may be gathered to form a complete student profile. Identification data come together to form a profile that outlines student skills and abilities, and this profile helps teachers and administrators make the most appropriate decisions regarding academic services for students. Familiarizing yourself with both the qualitative and quantitative criteria for gifted services in your school will help you develop a more in-depth understanding of the specific skills or potential to develop advanced skills for which students are identified as gifted. Many times, gifted teachers are actively involved in the student identification process, and this insight clarifies exactly how your students wound up in your classroom. If you are not aware of the type(s) of assessments your district uses for gifted identification, reach out to a campus leader or program coordinator to learn more. Understanding how and for what, specifically, students are identified will support your subsequent instructional decisions.

Common quantitative assessments include achievement tests, such as the Measures of Academic Progress (MAP), Iowa Assessments (formerly the Iowa Test of Basic Skills, or ITBS), the Test of Mathematical Abilities for Gifted Students (TOMAGS), the Screening Assessment for Gifted Elementary Students (SAGES), and other assessments similar to the SATs. Achievement tests help determine what students have already learned and how advanced they are compared to other students in their grade level (NAGC, n.d.-b). Your school may also make use of state testing data, but please observe some caution when using achievement tests with ceilings. This type of test does not allow students to show all of what they know, so if you are using this data, they should be in conjunction with other quantitative pieces.

Another type of quantitative assessment is the ability test. An ability test differs slightly from an achievement test, in that ability tests measure cognitive skills and abilities

CONSIDERING WAYS IN WHICH EDUCATORS CAN CAPTURE THE UNIQUE ABILITIES OF THESE CULTURALLY, LINGUISTICALLY, AND ECONOMICALLY DIVERSE (CLED) STUDENTS IS ESSENTIAL IN ESTABLISHING EQUITABLE IDENTIFICATION PRACTICES.

and can be used to identify potential and predict future success. Some common ability tests include IQ assessments, The Naglieri Nonverbal Ability Test (NNAT), the Cognitive Abilities Test (CogAT), the Otis Lennon Scholastic Ability Test (OLSAT), the Torrance Test of Creative Thinking, and the Raven's Progressive Matrices assessment. Including both achievement and ability data in a gifted student's profile helps to illustrate current achievement and future potential, or ability. As the gifted teacher, knowing exactly what your students' scores mean can help you identify key areas to develop, areas that need acceleration opportunities, and areas in which your students may need scaffolded support.

In conjunction with quantitative assessment data, many gifted scholars and practitioners advocate for the use of qualitative components in the identification process. Earlier, I discussed the role of referrals or nominations in the beginning phase of the identification process. These often take the form of surveys or scales, with open-ended parts, that the referring party completes. Although many times these documents do have quantitative scores, the opportunity to provide feedback on specific student attributes is also available. This provides both quantitative and qualitative information at the outset of identification.

During the assessment phase, portfolios, dynamic assessments such as performance-based tasks, auditions (Pfeiffer & Blei, 2008), classroom observations, and student interviews can be leveraged in order to provide additional evidence of specific advanced skills, motivation, and creativity. Having information that shines a light on actual student application and performance helps to create more equitable opportunities for identification, and also provides students with a more open opportunity to exemplify nonacademic exceptionalities, such as leadership and creativity. Used in tandem, qualitative and quantitative measures can build a well-rounded profile for the identification of gifted students.

In discussing identification, talking about the concept of equity is crucial. Many of the assessment procedures and metrics listed in this chapter effectively capture high performance and potential; however, students coming from economically disadvantaged backgrounds, those who have had limited access to early childhood learning opportunities, and students coming from culturally and linguistically diverse households may not perform as well on certain assessments. This performance gap certainly does not indicate a lack of potential, and considering ways in which educators can capture the unique abilities of these culturally, linguistically, and economically diverse (CLED) students is essential in establishing equitable identification practices.

If your district has a high population of students coming from economically and socially disadvantaged backgrounds, or if many of your students are English language learners (ELLs), carefully consider how appropriate your current identification metrics are in allowing these students to demonstrate potential. Are assessments available in students' native languages? Are there opportunities to assess nonverbal competencies, so that language is not a barrier? Do students have the appropriate academic foundation to do well on assessments? If you see that there are disproportionalities between students identified as gifted and the overall student demographic of your school (e.g., most of your gifted students are White, but your overall student body is largely Hispanic), that is a topic to be addressed with your administration team and program coordinators. Equity in identification and assessment is a basic educational right of which our students should be assured, and the gifted teacher can be a powerful advocate.

A key thing to remember in terms of identification is that your systems and measures should be robust enough to capture a variety of student abilities. Flexibility and openness when looking at data help to ensure that your identification practices support equity and serve to paint as whole of a picture of a student as possible. Some students take tests very well and will knock quantitative measures out of the park. However, remember that any test is a snapshot of what a child can do at one time—some students may not demonstrate their abilities appropriately on tests.

In working with gifted students and their families, I frequently hear parents reflect that the assessments used for identification did not adequately capture their child's abilities. In these cases, utilizing a different type of assessment, including performance-based tasks, and talking through student thinking and approaches to thinking and learning can really shine a light on skills not captured by the standard rounds of assessment. Students demonstrate advanced mathematical ability, read, write, and discuss literature well above grade level, and get an opportunity to really show their thinking when we assess from different angles. Other times, educators see that the original assessments were pretty accurate. Do not be afraid to dig a little deeper and be flexible in terms of using strengths-based measures to supplement identification data if there is an appropriate need. Please let me be clear: Maintaining standardization in assessment is important—a well-defined baseline and established criteria for providing academic services are critical in properly identifying and placing students in gifted services. However, when a case warrants deeper investigation, allow for students to demonstrate their abilities in ways that speak to their strengths and give insight into what they may actually be able to do in a gifted classroom.

Services

Much like identification practices, gifted and talented services take many different forms and structures from school to school. From push-in and pull-out programs, to magnet schools and gifted academies, to specially designated gifted classrooms, there are numerous ways in which gifted students have their academic needs met during the school day. Previous chapters discussed models for programming and some of the ways in which these models are implemented. You have also learned how all of the offerings available to gifted students come together through the Unified Program Design model to form a complete view of all services available to students. This section discusses strategies that ensure services meet programmatic goals, best align services with identification, and engage all stakeholders in order to increase knowledge and support of gifted programming schoolwide.

How Effective Are Our Services?

In order to be purposeful in making decisions related to gifted services, go all of the way back to the goals outlined for your program. How are these goals measured? If your goal is simply to be compliant with state or local mandates about the provision of gifted services, measurement is straightforward: compliant or not compliant. Beyond this, many programs seek to provide a differentiated academic experience for students identified as gifted in order to support increased achievement outcomes. Student achievement, exemplified through the generation of advanced products or performances and creative productivity, requires several structural supports, including attention to social and emotional development. Although your gifted program goals may be more specific or include multiple aspects of giftedness, most educators can agree that providing gifted students with access to learning opportunities that facilitate advanced outcomes is a major component of the why behind gifted education. This sounds grounded in common sense, right? Identify students, provide them with the differentiated experiences they need to be successful, and monitor their growth and achievement. This relatively straightforward, clear mission and process can get muddled at times and requires us to readjust and refocus our view.

> STUDENT OUTCOMES, INCLUDING ACADEMIC ACHIEVEMENT AND SOCIAL AND EMOTIONAL DEVELOPMENT, SHOULD BE THE DRIVERS BEHIND CREATION AND EVALUATION OF SERVICES.

A study conducted by Callahan, Moon, and Oh (2017) revealed that although a large number of district coordinators reported that their program's main goals centered around offering differentiated learning opportunities and instructional practices for gifted students, measurement of process goals (i.e., professional development, identification practices, and curriculum development) was used to guide and evaluate programming. If goals are student-focused, then it follows that product goals, such as student outcomes and achievement, should be driving services. A focus on the process with little to no attention paid to the product can result in services that aren't as student-focused as they could be. When you work with your campus and district leaders to discuss programming, absolutely use the opportunity to talk about what type(s) of training you've attended and how teachers receive support. Discuss effectiveness and equity in identification procedures. Spend time looking at whether or not resources have been allocated to secure quality instructional materials so that the student achievement outcomes reflect the goals of your program. The last part of that sentence should be what you spend the most time reflecting on, as it is crucial in ensuring that your services put the students at the forefront of decision making. Only then will you be able to advocate for possible programmatic changes and improvements with a clear and student-driven rationale. Student outcomes, including academic achievement and social and emotional development, should be the drivers behind creation and evaluation of services. The standard teaching practice of planning lessons with end goals in mind translates seamlessly into reflecting on and refining gifted services, and also helps to facilitate productive conversations about making changes or additions to the structures in place in order to help gifted students grow and develop. When advanced student achievement outcomes are the clear goals, the structure and alignment of gifted programs become significantly stronger.

ADDRESSING STUDENT OUTCOMES

Student outcomes can be addressed and evaluated in a number of ways. The most straightforward is through evaluating a student's grades, particularly if your school offers designated gifted classes. Of course, grades need to be evaluated in the context of the overall well-being of the student (i.e., Could behavior affect grades? Are there secondary issues that warrant attention?), but on the whole, how well a student performs in a gifted classroom is one indicator of whether or not services meet academic needs. If your service design does not include designated gifted classrooms, but does include work done in the general education classroom or collaboration between the general education and gifted teacher (push-ins, extension activities, etc.), grades may still be a useful component to examine, but only in the context of the type of services offered. For example, a student's reading grade will not be impacted by opportunities for accelerated math and should not be used to determine whether or not gifted services are effective for that student. If one is to use student grades as a way to measure outcomes, one must only consider the grades that provision of services directly impacts. You cannot expect gifted students to ace all material across all content areas. Use grades to measure student outcome only if those grades can be tied directly to the types of gifted services provided.

Gifted services that allow students to develop original products and engage in interdisciplinary learning, and are ongoing in nature, may effectively be monitored through the use of portfolios. Maintaining portfolios that show how students have developed their talents is also useful in monitoring student outcomes. Increasingly complex and sophisticated demonstrations of learning that are not necessarily linked to a grade can be kept in a portfolio, which follows students throughout the school year. The portfolio may well even carry over several years as students progress through the gifted program. Portfolios can be maintained as hard copies of student work, including photographs, reflections, and work logs, or digitally through a variety of platforms. As with most portfolios, choosing what is included should be done largely by the student, although the teacher may certainly add specific components. Portfolios are a great tool for documenting student outcomes, particularly when your service design does not necessarily result in established formal evaluation.

Many schools also provide gifted students with the opportunity to showcase their products to the wider community. Opportunities that allow students to share their work with authentic audiences are also effective ways for students to demonstrate advanced achievement. The key here is authenticity—if students are working on activities that address real problems or are interest-focused, then the audience should reflect that particular demographic. If younger students work on projects in which they think like disciplinarians and build specific academic skills in order to be thinkers and problem solvers, then an authentic audience would include school leadership, teachers, parents, and relevant community stakeholders. Older students may work with mentors outside of school, learn through concurrent enrollment in university classes or extension programs, or reach out to leaders to address and solve local or global problems. An authentic audience for these students would include members of the fields addressed through the project, teachers in their school, and others in academia. If your gifted services encourage independent or project-based learning, a good opportunity for students to showcase their work could be through a student-organized maker fair or project showcases.

The ways in which students can demonstrate their learning are numerous and should be specific to the nature of the learning activities. If you choose to monitor student outcomes through opportunities to share with an authentic audience, projects should not be forced, students should not be made to feel as if they are performing, and showcases with all of the earmarks of a dog-and-pony show should be avoided. Again, being student-focused here is key. Look to examples set by other special programs, such as English as a second language (ESL) family learning nights and Special Olympics. The focus in both examples is student learning and development, and opportunities for gifted students to share their outcomes should be no different.

Identification, services, and outcomes come together to form a reciprocal structure, with students at the center. Ensuring that identification practices are equitable, accessible, and effective results in a group of students who need quality services to develop their talents. When those services align tightly to identification practices, programs offer students highly effective learning experiences that directly target their areas of giftedness. Focusing on student achievement outcomes and monitoring growth mean that teachers and instructional leaders can be proactive, as well as meet student needs on the fly. This process of refining and reflecting on practices is recursive. It ensures that your program is focused but dynamic and responsive to the changing needs of students and families.

SUPPORT

Supporting gifted students and their families is an integral part of a high-quality gifted program. Engaging programmatic and student-specific support requires a few partnerships: partnerships with general education teachers, special education and ESL teachers, as well as instructional leaders and administration. Although you may sometimes feel like you are on an island in teaching gifted, your students certainly are not. When they walk out of the doors of your classroom, many students also receive services through other special programs, learn differently in other classrooms, and impact school culture in a variety of ways. Supporting both the students and your program is a big job that cannot be done in isolation.

GeneRAL EDUCATION TeACHeRS

Are you the only gifted teacher on your campus? Is there a disconnect between gifted and general education classrooms? Do you have difficulty collaborating with other teachers or teams because your content differs significantly than that of the general education classes? Making the time and forming the relationships necessary for collaboration may be tough, but do so anyways. This is not to say that you should be pushy or invasive and run the risk of alienating other teachers, but making a concerted effort to be a part of planning with other teachers on your campus can pay off exponentially.

If you provide a specialized pull-out or standalone gifted class, attending planning sessions and team meetings with teachers across grade levels and content areas can open your eyes to resources and strategies to support your students that you may have otherwise not thought about. Reaching out to collaborate also makes your role on campus more transparent, and the number of times you'll hear grumblings like, "It's easy to teach when you can do whatever you want," or, "Sure, you can do that; you have all the smart kids," will reduce significantly. Share struggles with your content or about student behavior and seek solutions. Show teachers how learning in their classroom impacts learning in your classroom.

In my experience coaching general education and gifted teachers, I noticed so many parallels in the types of questions and concerns both parties had for students: "So-and-so isn't finishing their work," "We're really struggling with this specific concept," and "I planned this whole lesson and it just completely fell apart. I don't know what to do." Being able to provide the general education teacher with insight about what was useful in a gifted classroom for a particular student, or sharing an effective reteach strategy from a general education classroom with a gifted teacher equipped everyone with new strategies—just imagine if that happened regularly! Sharing the content and planning that went on in the gifted classroom also quickly dispelled any thoughts of, "Students just go in there and play when they leave my classroom." Striking up a supportive relationship between gifted and regular classroom teachers can only pay out in dividends for students, and will certainly make the teachers' work easier.

In a collaborative relationship with general education teachers, you can better align content in the gifted classroom to help students make connections between classes. In addition to asking for insight into their classrooms, you can use this time together to provide strategies and resources that students can use outside of the gifted class. You can share with the teachers the types of academic scaffolding that go on in the gifted classroom, as well as the strategies you use to manage behavior (and yes, you definitely experience behavior problems!). Ask to attend these meetings or planning sessions, show up with questions about students and content, bring a resource or two to share, and make an effort to identify areas for purposeful connections between the general

> **SHARE STRUGGLES WITH YOUR CONTENT OR ABOUT STUDENT BEHAVIOR AND SEEK SOLUTIONS.**

education and gifted classrooms. If you cannot find a common planning time, you may consider requesting the opportunity to visit some of your students' classrooms for peer observations or rearranging your schedule to make visiting with general education teachers a priority.

There will be so many aha moments you share when you make time to plan together. For example, you might come to understand why a student misbehaves in your class but not in her homeroom teacher's class, realize that you do not need to do as much foundational instruction on a certain lesson as you thought, learn that so-and-so's parents never respond to e-mail and it is better to call, or realize that there are so many opportunities to work smarter, not harder, when you work together. Reaching out and asking to attend planning sessions with other teachers can be difficult, and it is an investment in time. But once collaboration with the gifted teacher becomes the norm and everyone can see the payoffs in student outcomes, all parties involved will see that it is well worth the effort.

SPECIAL PROGRAMS TEACHERS

Many students, in addition to receiving gifted services, also benefit from special education supports. These students fall under the twice-exceptional (2e) umbrella. According to data from the National Education Association (NEA, 2006), approximately 6% of the student population can be defined as twice-exceptional. These 2e students require flexible, customized supports and services (Coleman & Gallagher, 2015), and the gifted teacher is an integral part of the team that provides these services. We will discuss working with 2e students in depth in a later chapter, but it is worth noting here that in order to maximize these students' potential, teachers must collaborate. Partnerships with other special programs teachers, whether with a dyslexia therapist, an inclusion teacher, or a team of aides, give all parties involved the resources necessary to support student success.

Collaboration between gifted teachers and other special programs teachers helps students in a number of ways. First, open communication about student needs provides all teachers with a whole view of each child. Although all special programs seek to develop student abilities and talents in some way, the capacities and capabilities immediately evident in a special education classroom, for example, may not be so readily observable in the gifted classroom. Sometimes giftedness can mask manifestations of disabilities and vice versa (more on this later), so although the student is the same, the proficiencies observed in the gifted versus special education settings may be very different. A partnership between special programs teachers allows all parties with a vested academic interest in the students to share insight and observations with one another in order to get a full picture of what students can do and how they can grow.

Another benefit of working with other special programs teachers includes gaining strategies and resources to serve students. Gifted teachers may be doing their best to creatively and meaningfully implement the accommodations outlined in a student's Individualized Education Program (IEP) or 504 document, but are otherwise unaware of simple strategies or resources that provide effective supports for the student. Are there specific cues being used in other classrooms that help the student focus? Exactly how often does the student need reminders to stay on task? Working closely with the special education team will give answers and insight into what works best for students. Along these same lines, although special education teachers may be aware that a student is gifted, they may not be aware of the implications that this can have to the services they provide. Perhaps the student lags behind in meeting his or her academic or behavioral goals in special education services because the academic content is not provided at an appropriate level, which results in the student not completing work, as well as disruptive behavior. Sharing examples of what the students can do

> **OPEN COMMUNICATION ABOUT STUDENT NEEDS PROVIDES ALL TEACHERS WITH A WHOLE VIEW OF EACH CHILD.**

when provided a rigorous academic challenge can be very helpful to a special education teacher. A partnership with other special programs teachers can provide everyone involved with new tools, resources, and understandings to better meet the needs of each student.

Finally, open lines of communication and reflection between all special programs teachers help facilitate a strengths-based approach to educating the 2e student. A strengths-based approach to education simply means that teachers leverage student strengths to facilitate learning. Although this sounds simple, it is a process that requires individualization, networking, and deliberate application (Lopez & Loius, 2009). For example, a student with dyslexia may not be making satisfactory progress in either gifted classes or dyslexia therapy services because the texts used in therapy are too low-level and not engaging, but the texts in the gifted class may be at a frustration level for the student in terms of his or her ability to read what is on the page. Through collaboration between special programs teachers, the gifted teacher may share that this particular student is very interested in space and has an extensive knowledge of the topic. The dyslexia therapist can provide specific resources for breaking up and manipulating text that makes it more accessible for the student to read, which will reduce student frustration in the gifted classroom. In turn, the gifted teacher can give the dyslexia therapist examples of texts that are appropriately challenging and interesting to the student. Although the changes in both classrooms may be minimal, the impact for the student is significant. The student will no longer spend time in two separate classes being bored and frustrated. Instead, the student will have opportunities to learn and grow his or her skills in a way that is appropriate for his or her abilities.

Ongoing collaboration with other special programs teachers is something that requires intentionality, time, and ongoing effort. These investments will yield significant gains for the students, as well as an expanded skill set and tool kit for teachers. Having IEP documents and accommodations to reference is a great starting point, but they are not enough when it comes to developing student talent in the long term.

ADMINISTRATION

A positive and open relationship with your administrative team is essential in making sure gifted services receive adequate support. Creating and maintaining this relationship may take some work on the part of the teacher, because many times, "gifted students are not the primary focus since they most often meet proficiency standards and do not have as urgent needs as other students" (Johnsen, 2013). If gifted students and services are not an important blip on your administrators' radars because they are not perceived as a high-need student group, or simply due to lack of knowledge regarding gifted education, you may need to put in some extra effort in making sure the program gets the attention and resources to make it successful.

In a study on the preparation of school leadership regarding special programs, McHatton, Boyer, Shaunessy, Terry, and Farmer (2010) found that the majority of administrators reported that their preparation program had no courses relating to gifted and talented services. Moreover, professional development directly related to gifted services provided to leaders by school districts was minimal and focused more on the legal and financial obligations versus the nature and needs of gifted learners. This simply means that you and your administrators may be learning about best practices for gifted students together, and that as you advocate for resources and services, you may need to help your leadership gain a deeper understanding of the why behind gifted programming, through respectful conversation and collaboration.

In her work on addressing the challenge of administrator support, Johnsen (2013) said that there are three key areas in which advocates of gifted services should focus: (1) dispelling the myths surrounding gifted education, (2) illustrating how many of the strategies used in gifted education can benefit all students, and (3) describing the ways in which structures and resources may be leveraged for gifted education without additional costs.

Regarding the first point, NAGC (n.d.-a) created a list of myths about gifted students that could be helpful in facilitating proactive conversation with your administrative leaders. These myths include the notions that gifted students will do fine on their own, teachers can provide appropriate challenge for gifted students in the regular classroom, gifted students should be role models for others, all children are gifted, acceleration opportunities are socially harmful for gifted students, gifted programs are elitist, students can't be gifted if they get bad grades, all gifted students are well-adjusted, students cannot be gifted if they have a disability, Advanced Placement (AP) courses should meet the needs of gifted students without additional services, and gifted programs are expensive and require lots of resources. Equipping yourself with the knowledge and resources needed to dispel these myths through open and proactive conversation with administration is certainly a great first step in building a positive relationship with the instructional leaders in your school.

The second and third points can be addressed in tandem. We know that the differentiation practices, particular attention paid to learning needs, and the flexibility needed to let students learn at a respectful and appropriate pace are good for all students, period. When

> **STUDENT CHOICE SIMPLY PROVIDES OPTIONS FOR INDIVIDUALS TO TAKE OWNERSHIP OF THEIR WORK.**

providing resources like professional development or auxiliary classroom materials, effective schools select resources that can be scaffolded up and down so that they reach all learners. The types of differentiation suggested for gifted learners—that is, flexible pacing, appropriately leveled learning material, and student choice—are no different than what we would want for every single student in our schools. For some students, pacing is slowed; for gifted students, it may be accelerated. Some students may need learning material that is at or below grade level; gifted students many times need advanced material. Student choice simply provides options for individuals to take ownership of their work.

Differentiation strategies that meet these needs, such as menus, tiered instruction, flexible grouping, and independent learning contracts, are good for all students, not just gifted. This point goes hand-in-hand with Johnsen's (2013) third point: Effective gifted services can be creatively developed in ways that are not costly. Gifted services do not necessarily need flashy bells and whistles to meet student needs. Thoughtful considerations, such as cluster grouping, scheduling to accommodate gifted services, providing consistent and adequate spaces for gifted classes to take place, and including gifted in the overall academic community and future school plans are steps in the right direction. These efforts require no additional monetary cost, nor do they take away from any other initiative or priority.

Establishing gifted programs that are designed to explicitly meet the needs of the school's advanced learners benefits the entire school in a number of ways. Gifted services provide relief for and shared responsibility with general education teachers by including a gifted support person. This way, meeting the unique needs of every single student in the classroom is not one person's sole responsibility. Rather, faculty members get an extra head and hands in making sure gifted students get what they need to be successful every day. Carefully designed and maintained gifted services also help ensure that students with high levels of potential are able to achieve and make gains similar to that of their grade-level peers. Fostering an environment that supports equitable development opportunities for all facilitates an overall campus culture of high achievement. These are both wins for the whole school.

Working with administration is a crucial part of developing and sustaining an effective system of services for gifted students. Depending on your administrators' level of familiarity with gifted students and programs, you may be learning about what best meets your advanced learners' needs as you go, together. As the gifted teacher, your responsibility is to be informed, proactive, and communicative with school leadership regarding gifted services. This may be a process, but helping administrators understand the why and the benefits associated with supporting gifted services is key in making sure students get the academic opportunities and experiences they need to grow.

PUTTING IT ALL TOGETHER

The reciprocal roles of identification, services, and support are critical components of gifted services. As a new teacher, you may be overwhelmed as you determine how these moving parts come together to build an effective program for students. But this elephant is to be eaten one bite at a time. Begin with making sure you have a functional knowledge of each piece and grow from there. It may take several years to get things where you want them to be, and that is perfectly okay. As long as the students are at the center of your decision making and they continue to benefit from the vision, innovation, and hard work put into developing effective programs, then you are successfully fulfilling your role as a teacher and advocate.

CHAPTER 4

PARENTS AND COMMUNITY ENGAGEMENT

Building and strengthening the connections between parent, student, and community is vital to any successful classroom. Parents of gifted students often have unique questions, concerns, and interests regarding their students, and conversations can become difficult. As a gifted teacher, you may be faced with questions and concerns from families that you have not encountered before. Being able to anticipate the types of inquiries parents may reach out with and developing strategies with which you can approach these interactions will be helpful as you navigate the new waters of gifted education.

For any teacher, engaging parents and community stakeholders is important from the beginning so that you establish clear lines of communication. Openness to collaboration and communication will make difficult conversations easier, and bolstering support for students, even if the parties have differing ideas, will be helpful. Although this is a general best practice, building and fostering relationships outside of the school will serve your gifted students in ways that you may not expect. Skillfully and proactively engaging parents and other community stakeholders can help to widen the impact of gifted services, develop networks of advocates for gifted programming, and cultivate resources for student learning outside of the classroom.

BUILDING PARENT-TEACHER RELATIONSHIPS

Parent-teacher relationships are distinctly different than parent involvement. Parent involvement includes behaviors that support students (i.e., volunteering at school, providing learning opportunities at home), whereas the parent-teacher relationship focuses more on the connection between students' home supports (parents, guardians) and school personnel. Healthy parent-teacher relationships are trusting, respectful, mutually supportive, characterized by accountability, and hold the student at the center of ongoing collaboration (Minke, Sheridan, Kim, Ryoo, & Koziol, 2014). A key difference is that parents can be heavily involved in their child's education with very little, passive, or only reactive participation from the teacher. You want to cultivate a two-way street of feedback and support with parents. This cooperative connection between teachers and parents will create a shared responsibility for helping students achieve their academic goals (Penney & Wilgosh, 2000). Building a strong relationship with parents or guardians creates a network of student support and ultimately seeks to help students maximize their potential.

ENGAGEMENT STRATEGIES

Parent-teacher relationships build a partnership between school and home, the level of school engagement of parents, and the comfort with which the teacher feels in communicating, in addition to supporting the student's academic experience (Buhl & Hilkenmeier, 2017). But what do you do when parents are difficult to reach or engage? On the flip side, what do you do when parents are overly eager to engage and you can't ever seem to give them enough of your time and attention? This section examines some strategies that can help draw out your reluctant or hard-to-reach parents, as well as ways to proactively communicate and establish healthy boundaries with those eager parents.

If parent relationships are difficult to initiate in your school, ask yourself why. Parent-teacher relationship quality effectively predicts and encourages parental involvement, which directly impacts the student's academic experience. However, minority and less educated parents have shown to be less involved in school than White or more educated families (Nzinga-Johnson, Baker, & Aupperlee, 2009). Although there are several significant social, economic, cultural, and political factors that underlie this issue, this section focuses on identifying more common problems and solutions to make school more inclusive for all families of gifted students.

Are parents working multiple jobs, with few opportunities to engage with their student's school? Is transportation an issue? Do parents who are not English speakers know how to or feel comfortable requesting meetings with translators? Are there cultural expectations or beliefs about school that may interfere with open two-way communication? Chances are, if this is an issue in your school, you are not the only teacher frustrated by this problem. Rather than try to tackle this problem alone, reach out to other teachers and administration to look for opportunities to partner up and support one another's efforts to reach parents.

Consider holding joint conferences with other teachers if parents have limited time. You could work in a small group for a round robin-style conference if this maximizes the parents' time. A word of caution, if

> **SHOW PARENTS THAT YOU ARE CONSCIENTIOUS AND RESPECTFUL OF THEIR LIMITED TIME, AND THEY WILL CERTAINLY APPRECIATE THE CONSIDERATION.**

using this method: Work out talking points beforehand so no one teacher dominates the conversation. Ensure that everyone's feedback focuses on growth and potential, as well as thoughts about new strategies, so you avoid a situation where the parent feels like teachers are ganging up on him or her. If you need to have a confidential conversation with the parent, see if you can leverage the student's teacher team to help cover one another's classes. If there is only a specific time when parents come in when you are otherwise busy, this may be the only way to make a meeting happen.

If parents are simply too busy or have limited time to devote to school activities, try hosting events that allow them to accomplish multiple tasks. Holding a potluck, for example, gives working parents an opportunity to feed themselves and their kids while spending time with the teacher. If your school offers activities like family literacy nights or hosts an extended school day, work with your administration to be a part of these activities to give parents an opportunity to connect with you. If travel is unreliable or too time consuming to get to their student's schools, offer to meet parents at an alternative location. (I would strongly suggest that you select the location carefully and include another teacher in the meeting so that you can observe safety precautions.) If your school has a social worker, reach out to him or her in specific cases of particularly hard-to-contact parents to see if he or she can share effective engagement strategies. Show parents that you are conscientious and respectful of their limited time, and they will certainly appreciate the consideration.

If parents do not speak the predominant language of the school fluently, they may also be less likely to engage with teachers. Parents who are English language learners should always have the option of having an interpreter, who is not their child, available. Your school's student management database can likely show if the student's family speaks another language predominantly at home. Otherwise, if you are unsure, just ask. Another teacher or administrator may be able to give you some insight here. You could also ask the parent directly. However, there is a clear difference between being respectful and accessible, and assuming based on someone's race alone that he or she does not speak the language proficiently. When preparing for a conference, letting parents know that there is a translator available if they would like to use one is respectful. You may also ask parents if they are attending the conference alone, or if someone else is joining them. Many times, a parent will bring another family member or friend to assist with language if needed, and simply asking if anyone else is coming is a good way for you to anticipate this and plan accordingly. It is not respectful to assume that parents will need a translator if they are not native speakers of your school's predominant language. Making sure that families know that interpretation services are readily available, should they choose to use them, is important in ensuring the comfort of the parent and the opportunity for clear, two-way communication.

Reluctant parents can also be engaged through home visits. If parents are reticent to visit the school due to cultural expectations or beliefs about school and the role of the teacher, you may put the ball in their court, so to speak, by meeting them in their home. Make it clear that you are coming just to meet them, keep conversation limited to opportunities at school, and share a positive goal for their student (Lin & Bates, 2010). These meetings should be less formal and seek to put parents at ease. You may also be able to observe your students in a different setting that could shed light on their behaviors at school. Home visits work to strengthen the bond between families and schools (Kronholz, 2016) through making the teacher an accessible figure, not necessarily an authoritarian. Home visits also show families that you are willing and interested to learn more about them as individuals and demonstrates that you have a vested interest in their student's overall success. This also gives families a chance to share their cultures and backgrounds, which helps to establish a relation based on trust and mutual respect.

In contrast to reluctant parents, you may also have overly eager parents who seem to make constant demands on your time and attention. These parents may come across in such a way because they feel that they lack the information they need to support their student in being successful at school. Their eagerness is a desire to understand what is going on in school and form a partnership. Many times, proactive communication can help give parents the insight and resources they need to feel supported. Before the year begins (or as early on as you are able), share clearly established goals for your gifted classes. Something as simple as a photo of your classroom norms after the first few days of school, with an accompanying blurb about setting these norms to meet gifted classroom goals, makes the classroom more accessible, gives parents talking points with their students, and creates transparency. Providing parents with calendars of activities and specific learning objectives (in parent-friendly language), as well as ongoing feedback regarding classroom activities, helps to give a regular, steady dose of the information they're seeking. Providing parents with regular resources and activities to do outside of the classroom also gives parents a voice and active role in the education partnership. In creating these communication and sharing networks for parents, leverage technology to help keep everyone connected. Google Classroom, platforms such as Seesaw, and regular electronic newsletters are great places to start, and are easy to maintain. Classroom and learning-oriented communication also puts student achievement at the center of the conversation, which is important in assuring that the parent-teacher relationship is focused squarely around the student's success.

These suggestions are simply that: suggestions. The most important thing to remember in connecting with parents is that every situation is unique. Show parents that you are willing and want to understand their situation and come up with supports that meet their needs. This might mean getting creative with your time or meeting formats, but that effort will definitely pay off in the relationships you are able to build.

CONNECTING WITH PARENTS OF GIFTED STUDENTS

Having a positive, proactive relationship with parents is key. I learned this the hard way during my first year teaching gifted learners. I was responsible for K–8 pull-outs, on top of a full load teaching two different grade levels, so I was stretched pretty thin. One parent of a gifted student frequently sent me e-mails about how my recent instruction was subpar, or a particular way I had damaged their child's learning for the week. This parent would also hang out in the front lobby and take any opportunity to catch me at dismissal to provide feedback about their child's distaste for a lesson we'd done that week. In one of our many exchanges, the accusation that I was "destroying the child's love of learning" came up. To say that this parent had me frazzled and doubting myself is an understatement. This particular child was also transitioning from elementary to middle school, which many of you know is a sticky time period in which cute elementary kids turn into tweens. In this fun new phase, parents are no longer as important to the students, new behaviors and attitudes crop up, and overall academic demands at school increase significantly. Looking back, I can see that this parent was just as frustrated as I was. In the time it took me to respond to e-mails or talk in the lobby, I could have communicated our units in advance, leveraged that parent for help at school (I needed it!), and provided the parent with meaningful homeschool connections. This parent just wanted to be a part of their child's learning and probably needed affirmation from another adult that what they were experiencing, in terms of their student's development, was normal. Hindsight is 20/20, and it is easy for me to reflect on the unspoken needs that this parent had now. But at the time, the situation caused us both (the parent and me) undue stress. This was a missed opportunity on my part. I share this story not to perpetuate the stereotype of the over-the-top parent of a gifted student, or to place the responsibility of establishing positive relationships solely on the teacher, but to illustrate how stepping back and asking yourself what a parent really needs can save everyone tears and time, and lay the groundwork for a strong home-school relationship.

Many times, parents of gifted students get a bad rap as pushy, overbearing, and perfectionistic. They may be thought of like the parent from my story, always sending e-mails, questioning everything you do, bombarding you with "helpful" suggestions, and going above your head to an administrator any time a problem arises. Many of these "helicopter" or "lawnmower parents" stereotypes are simply untrue, or not specific to parents of gifted students. However, the gifted teacher faces unique parent needs and concerns, and must provide specific supports in order to do his or her part to facilitate a positive teacher-parent relationship. Many times, these parents are reaching out to find answers and get feedback on their students, whose abilities and behaviors may be such that parents are left stumped and wondering how to help their child.

Gifted children many times speak and comprehend advanced language early, which can lead to the development of complex concepts and skills well above what is age-typical (McGee & Hughes, 2011). Although this precociousness may lend itself well to advanced learning and academic ability in school, it may have more long-term and ongoing impacts in the home. Early skill development and awareness of complex concepts could lead to fears, sensitivities, issues with self-esteem, and negative behaviors (McGee & Hughes, 2011) that parents have had to cope with for years, long before the student has reached your classroom. These parents may very well be reaching out to you for help, a lifesaver, or simply confirmation that these are indeed expected and typical behaviors for a gifted student, and that you can provide support. Connecting your parents with organizations in the community, state, and nation will provide them with another support network of which they otherwise may not have been aware.

> **ALL [PARENTS] BENEFIT FROM THE OPPORTUNITY TO GROW THEIR KNOWLEDGE ABOUT GIFTEDNESS AND STRATEGIES FOR WORKING WITH THEIR CHILDREN.**

Parents who are overeager may also be in defense mode from the get-go. Many gifted children spend a considerable amount of time in their regular classrooms hearing the same material, over and over, and are infrequently challenged at an appropriate level. This leads to general dislike of school, potential behavior issues, and frustrated parents who know that if their child had better academic opportunities, he or she could meet his or her full potential. In a study of student and parent perspectives on gifted education, Young and Balli (2014) found that not only were neighborhood schools inconsistent in the ways in which they met the needs of their gifted students, but also both student and parent respondents reported a desire for increased exposure to deeper knowledge and creative opportunities. Fighting this perceived battle of inconsistent or low-quality services year after year puts many parents immediately on the defensive in terms of relationships with teachers and the school. Again, listening to the whole story and doing your homework (conference with other teachers, be ready to speak to the student's performance in your class, examine data to look for trends, have some options or examples of advanced learning opportunities ready to share, etc.) will show parents that you are indeed on their team in terms of making sure their children get what they need to be successful.

Providing parents with a designated opportunity to connect with you, receive your undivided attention, and really be heard (including subtext of the conversation) is a good first step in establishing a positive relationship with parents of gifted students. Being able to have a shared perception of a high-quality parent-teacher relationship is important in supporting positive student outcomes (Minke et al., 2014). If persistent behavior continues, establishing clear boundaries—such as not answering e-mails sent at 10:30 p.m., choosing to respond or not to nonemergency calls and texts when you are at home, and ensuring your attention is equitably divided among your other families—is a helpful strategy that will show parents that you care, but there is a clear delineation between school and home.

Whether you encounter an unengaged parent, an engaged parent, or any parent of a gifted student in between, all benefit from the opportunity to grow their knowledge about giftedness and strategies for working with their children. Parent education workshops can be great offerings for your community of families. Weber and Stanley (2012) suggested the following considerations when setting up parent workshops at your school:

- collaborate with a sponsoring organization to help support the event itself;

- include professionals from the community (such as counselors and university faculty);
- make sure the event is well-publicized, and interpreters are available for the event;
- seek out funds to help minimize or eliminate any cost to families;
- choose a centralized, easy-to-reach location;
- consider transportation and childcare needs of families; and
- be mindful of conflicting events (sports, competitions, etc.).

In addition to providing the school-based supports that parents of gifted students need, empower parents with the knowledge that they need to strengthen the home component of the home-school connection. According to Rotigel (2003), when families are appropriately educated about what giftedness is and its implications for the whole child, parents may be more sensitive in their nurturing and can effectively advocate for their child with other adults and schools. Parent education programs provide essential information for families regarding how they can serve their child's needs in the family setting.

Opportunities for appropriate learning are key not only for student success, but for parents as well.

HARD CONVERSATIONS

Regardless of how proactive, open, and communicative you are, there will always be a need to have hard conversations with your students and their families. Teaching gifted children does not mean that there will be no problems with behavior or academics. In fact, behavioral and academic issues associated with gifted students should be expected. Although the roots of these problems and solutions may not be what you are used to dealing with, the fact is that kids are kids. They are learning how to navigate the world around them socially and emotionally, experiencing academic successes and failures, and developing coping strategies. A gifted label does not lessen or eliminate the struggles that all students face at some point or another. With these struggles often come hard conversations between the teacher and parent. There is no magic solution that will make hard conversations easier or less painful, but Whiteman (2013) shared some useful strategies for facilitating these discussions. When you meet with parents, engage in active listening. This means that you are focused on what the other party is saying, rather than mentally preparing a rebuttal, and then repeat back what you understood. This tells parents that they were heard, confirms that you understood what they meant, and allows them to reflect on and clarify their words. Active listening also includes reading body language and tone. As simple as this sounds, it is a great strategy to avoid conflict based on misunderstanding.

Being empathetic also helps parents feel understood and validated (Whiteman, 2013). When you empathize with them, let them know that you hear and understand what they are saying. This indicates that you acknowledge that their interpretation of the situation, which may lessen frustrated, upset, lost, or defeated feelings. You do not necessarily have to feel the same emotions as the parents (in all likelihood you will not share their emotions), but an empathetic listener takes the feelings of the other into account, and validates that they are real and difficult to reconcile.

> **A GIFTED LABEL DOESN'T LESSEN OR ELIMINATE THE STRUGGLES THAT ALL STUDENTS FACE AT SOME POINT OR ANOTHER.**

A third strategy for having hard conversations involves asking questions and wondering. Through questioning, you are communicating to parents that you acknowledge and respect their perspective. They are the expert on their child, and you value their insight. Wondering ("I wonder how this situation would change if we tried XYZ,") allows parents to be equal problem solvers and shows them that you value their feedback (Whiteman, 2013).

These are some general approaches one can use through the course of difficult conversations with parents. You simply cannot avoid the hard topics around which these conversations take place, but you can control how you respond. As with most students, hard conversations typically center around behavior and academics. These are areas in which students are learning and, as with all learning, will experience failure at some point or another. The next two sections look at some additional strategies, specific to behavior and academic-related issues.

BeHAVIOR

In a study of gifted students, Morawska and Sanders (2008) found that gifted students did not exhibit more behavioral difficulties than other nongifted peers. However, gifted children did show higher levels of behavior symptoms related to emotionality and peer relations. Compound this with the knowledge that gifted children can understand deep, complex ideas at an earlier age and may be attuned to emotional sensitivities, and you have the potential for a real behavior issue.

When partnering with parents to address behavior concerns, separate the behavior from the learning. Remember those parents from earlier in the chapter who were frustrated with the perceived consistencies and quality of learning opportunities appropriate for their students? Defensive parents may first try to claim that their student's behavior is a result of a lack of academic challenge. The student is bored, so he or she is baiting other kids or acting out. In preparation for meeting with parents, ask yourself honestly if this is true. If you know that it is not, be ready to provide the parents with concrete examples of behavior issues that occur when the student is appropriately academically engaged. Remind them that your concern here is the learning of their student and others in the class, and that it's normal and expected for students to struggle with behavior from time to time. Ask parents to reflect on what they notice at home and share strategies they find useful in managing behavior. Agree on strategies to correct the behavior at school, communicate both good and bad days regularly to parents, and set a time to come together again to reflect on progress.

Any time you are able, involve students in this process as well (to the degree that it is appropriate to their level of understanding). Making sure students have the opportunity to help root out the cause of the issue, and certainly assist in identifying the strategies they will use to take ownership and correct the problem, is another piece of the puzzle. If a student does not see that the redirection strategy, consequence, etc., reflects the behavior, your plan will likely fail. Focus the difficult conversation on the behavior, discuss only relevant external factors, and create a goal of meeting a specific success outcome for the student. Solicit feedback from both the student (once again, as appropriate) and the parent, and select concrete strategies for helping the student to reach the behavior goal. When leading these conversations, remember to structure the discussion in such a way that intelligence or ability is not tied directly to behavior ("You must not be as smart as everyone thinks you are if you're acting that way."), and parents can be assured that the issue isn't a byproduct of disengagement or boredom. Discussing behavior in a way that isolates problem issues, rather than painting a student with a "bad kid" image, is helpful in making sure the conversation stays focused and on track. This will help clear the path to have a productive conversation focused on positive outcomes.

ACADemICS

Failure is part of the learning process (Roberts & Lovett, 1994), and gifted students will inevitably experience the uncomfortable struggles and challenges that accompany it. The motivational, emotional, and attitudinal components that accompany failure are discussed in a later chapter; here, you will focus on the ways in which you can have open and honest conversations with parents about the topic. When a student encounters sustained challenge that results in failure, parents may be concerned for a number of reasons. Perhaps their child has reached his or her "peak" and parents are afraid that this means their child will not continue to grow academically. If a student struggles for an entire marking period or semester, parents may be concerned that their child is no longer gifted. Conversely, if the gifted classroom is no longer the best academic fit for the student, parents may be unwilling to talk about alternatives. Academic achievement can be a touchy area for gifted students and their families, and teachers should be ready to talk respectfully and openly about problems and solutions.

If parents become concerned that a struggle indicates the "end of the gifted rope," frame the difficulty that their student is experiencing around what it means to be academically successful. Students who are successful without effort are not experiencing academic challenges commensurate with their ability. A student who struggles and fails sometimes is learning; the real concern is when the pace of learning and development is mismatched with the pace of instruction in the class. As long as the student is able to master the concepts and objectives at a pace and level that matches that of the gifted classroom, then struggle and failure are perfectly acceptable. This does not mean that the student is not gifted; it means that the student has an opportunity to work hard to develop his or her talent in ways he or she may not have thought about yet. Encourage parents to accept struggle and failure while praising the work. Focusing on what students were not able to do and dismissing the effort that they put in to learn can create a "why try?" attitude or encourage perfectionistic tendencies.

> **A STUDENT WHO STRUGGLES AND FAILS SOMETIMES IS LEARNING.**

Students who seem to be encountering academic challenges for the first time may set off parental alarm bells. In this situation, assure parents that the rates at which students demonstrate growth can change as they get older. Students who experienced exponential academic growth in early elementary school may not grow as rapidly with their more complex content in middle school. This simply shows that students need to stretch their thinking muscles more actively in order to engage the analysis and synthesis skills they're developing. This certainly does not mean that students do not still have the potential to perform at gifted levels.

Difficult conversations also arise when the challenge of the gifted classroom is no longer an appropriate academic fit for students, and their learning needs should be met in the general education setting. If you are concerned that the gifted classroom might not be appropriate for a child for academic reasons, take the appropriate steps of intervening to help support the student, keep the parents in the loop about your concerns, and gather data exemplifying a mismatch between the student and his or her current placement. The "I don't know if the gifted program is right for your student" conversation should not be the first time that parents hear about academic concerns. This conversation should occur as the next step after all other attempts at support have been exhausted. In this situation, parents may deny the issue, point out isolated areas of strengths, or place blame on your instruction. Although these can be frustrating points for you as the teacher, keep the focus of the conversation on the student and his or her well-being.

Gifted services, like other special programs, are designed to meet advanced learning needs. When a student no longer demonstrates those needs, then it's time to consider a different placement. Help parents see that keeping a student in a class that is not academically appropriate will only widen his or her knowledge gaps because the content and pace do not match the student's ability. The student also likely feels frustrated, embarrassed, and could be experiencing negative self-efficacy—no one in the classroom feeling these feelings regularly is primed to learn. Remind parents that just because the student will not be in your class anymore does not mean you will stop supporting the child or the family. Reassure them that you will work with the general education teacher(s) to make the transition smooth, and you are happy to provide resources and strategies to that teacher in order to give the student more appropriate options in the classroom. Above all, keep the student's well-being at the center of the conversation. In situations when the topic of conversation is an exit from gifted services, make sure you have looped in your administration, too. Your part of this discussion is to help everyone work as a team to find the best fit for the student. The other members of this team, namely, the parents, may be reluctant, but helping them to see the long-term implications of an appropriate academic fit will help make this difficult conversation run a little more smoothly.

COMMUNITY ENGAGEMENT

A frequently overlooked group of people that can be great resources of advocacy and support is the community outside of school. Providing community stakeholders outside of the walls of your school with a glimpse into what happens in a gifted classroom and how they can partner to enrich the experiences of the students can build advocacy and understanding of gifted services within the community (Wiskow, Fowler, & Christopher, 2011). Making connections to the community surrounding your school is the next step, outside of the walls of your building, to generating knowledge and support of gifted services.

You can engage the community via relationships with parents—many parents would be eager to share people and resources from their jobs, cultural organizations, and outside interests to support student learning in the gifted classroom. You can also reach out to your local chamber of commerce, town council, colleges, and universities, as well as several other organizations in your community and invite them to be authentic audiences for your students' ideas and products. Forming relationships with businesses, schools, nonprofit organizations, and other community members can provide enrichment opportunities for students that they otherwise might not receive or know about (Nathan, 2015). Community partnerships create chances for students to make connections with audiences who can provide real-world, professional feedback on their learning and ideas, and facilitate mentorship opportunities. Thinking more globally, you can make contact with state and national bodies, as well as large-scale organizations that have education programs; many of these groups would be eager to work with the students in your classroom. Using online platforms makes bringing an expert or mentor into the classroom easy and accessible, and provides a wider array of options for students. This may be particularly helpful if you live in a rural area, where there are limited opportunities for face-to-face interactions. Whatever the scope or format, connecting students to real-world experiences and showing others outside of your school the potential that gifted services seeks to develop is a great way to add depth and diversity to the resources you offer your students.

Long-term results of positive community engagement include a "positive, inviting, and inclusive school culture" (Hains, Gross, Blue-Banning, Francis, & Turnbull 2015) and a storehouse of potential opportunities for students. When the community sees the value and meaning behind what students are doing in the gifted classroom, particularly when the learning activities generate creative solutions to real problems, the value of services becomes cemented in their idea of what the school does for its students. Gifted services move closer to the forefront of community members' minds when they think about what the school has to offer. Exposure to real-world, creative problem solving also gives students an idea

COMMUNITY PARTNERSHIPS CREATE CHANCES FOR STUDENTS TO MAKE CONNECTIONS WITH AUDIENCES WHO CAN PROVIDE REAL-WORLD, PROFESSIONAL FEEDBACK.

of how they can give back to their community, which is a great investment in the future growth and development of your neighborhood, city, or town. Connecting the learning that happens in the gifted classroom to the long-term development potential of the community shows stakeholders and students alike how valuable your program and services can be.

PARENTS AND THE COMMUNITY: BUILDING PARTNERSHIPS

Your classroom does not exist in a silo, on an island, or in a vacuum. Widen the scope of involvement, and consequently, the impact of your services to students, through creating networks of support through the parents and the community. Relationships both within the school and outside of its walls create openness, transparency, and a culture of understanding and mutual respect. These relationships do not form overnight, and like all valuable relationships, take time and effort. As a new gifted teacher, start with reasonable goals; for example, you will call three parents with positive feedback this week, and post a home activity to your Google Classroom or similar platform. Next, you may reach out to another teacher or two so that you may work together to get that difficult-to-reach parent in for a conference. After that, you might reach out to your local university to see if folks from a particular content area or department would like to visit your students and see what they've been working on. As you complete these networking acts, you will find your systems of support growing. By the end of the year, maybe your goals include conferencing with every parent at least once, engaging in an outside activity that involves students and families (i.e., visiting some students at home, attending a sports event where a number of your students are on a team, attending a cultural event in which your students take part), hosting an information session for parents, and having at least one outside guest in your classroom. This sounds like a lofty goal, but if you do these things in the course of a school year, these things are fairly attainable. The bottom line is this: You are not alone in your investment in your students' successes. Partner with those other invested parties—the parents and the community at large—and find out how working together can create great insight and opportunities for your students.

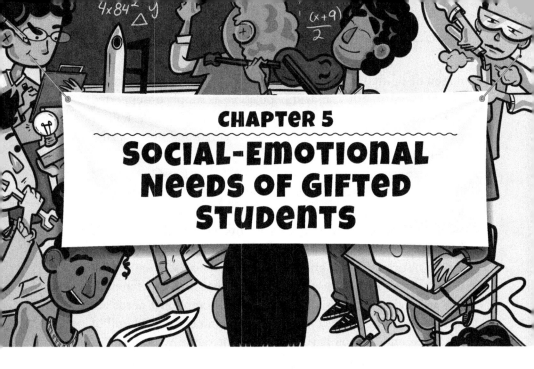

CHAPTER 5

SOCIAL-EMOTIONAL NEEDS OF GIFTED STUDENTS

Meeting the social and emotional needs of students is a topic that is quickly rising in popularity across all areas of education. Books and articles on issues associated with social and emotional well-being, along with tips and suggestions regarding how to include social-emotional learning (SEL) in the classroom, can be found across the field. In fact, one study identified more than 200 SEL programs available to schools today (Lawson, McKenzie, Becker, Selby, & Hoover, 2019). So, ready or not, expectations to address social-emotional needs in your classroom and in the school as a whole are coming. This chapter identifies social-emotional needs you may find prevalent among your gifted students, the why underlying these needs, and how you can implement specific classroom structures and practices to facilitate positive SEL experiences for your students.

When discussing the social-emotional needs of your gifted students, you need to understand that these students are as psychologically healthy as their age-level peers (Cross, 2009), as well adjusted as any other group of students (Neihart, Pfeiffer, & Cross, 2016), and generally do not face any additional social-emotional issues compared to other students (Reis & Renzulli, 2004). The notion that gifted students suffer from social-emotional issues at a higher rate than other student populations is simply unsupported by research. To view gifted students as emotionally fragile, frail, or prone to psychological dysfunction is inaccurate and simply a false stereotype.

When considering the social and emotional needs of gifted students, remember to examine their needs with a student-forward lens. That is, "these are gifted students who may need/feel/think. . ." versus labeling students as "anxious gifted kid" or "perfectionist." Just as you would not label a student by a disability, you should not characterize gifted students by their social-emotional needs. This will help you keep in mind that first and foremost you are dealing with children whose social-emotional needs are often dictated by their situation and environment, just like all of the other students you have likely encountered in your time as a teacher. Do educators find more of certain needs within gifted populations? Yes. Are these needs innately tied to the students themselves? Most current research says no. Giftedness itself does not create problems or distress in students, but the associated pressures, expectations, and personal beliefs may create some difficulty (Kennedy & Farley, 2018). With this in mind, look at some of the more prevalent social-emotional needs you may encounter.

ASYNCHRONOUS DEVELOPMENT

Asynchronous development is a term that means exactly what one would think: out-of-sync. That is, cognitive abilities, social awareness, and physical development differ from one another within an individual (Silverman, 1997), and some of these internal and external components are out of pace with one's peers. Recall the example of early language acquisition and development from a previous chapter. Gifted children may speak early, as well as understand advanced language and concepts (McGee & Hughes, 2011). If a young child can understand and discuss complex issues, such as social injustice, who can he or she have these conversations with at school . . . another 6-year-old? Probably not. That interaction would be strange and uncomfortable for both children, because one possesses understanding and communication skills that the other does not. This may lead gifted children to seek out adults or other older students for companionship, which could result in isolation from and difficulty connecting with their same-age peers.

Consider some additional examples: Your kindergarten student is a voracious reader and loves telling stories, but he or she struggles with the motor skills exercised in writing. This child becomes quickly frustrated that his or her body (i.e., the physical process of writing) cannot keep up with his or her mind (the story the student wishes to tell), and he or she becomes upset and disengages from the activity. Another student who is mathematically gifted may be able to cruise by in elementary school, never getting a problem incorrect or struggling with computation or problem solving. But as soon as the student encounters advanced middle school math, he or she starts getting problems

> **HIGH INTELLECT OR ACADEMIC ABILITY DOES NOT EQUAL ADVANCED-LEVEL SELF-AWARENESS OR REGULATORY ABILITY. THESE SKILLS NEED TO BE EXPLICITLY TAUGHT.**

wrong, making computational mistakes, and becomes confused by his or her lack of immediate mastery. If this student has not had to exercise the emotional regulatory structures used to deal with the stress and anxiety of academic difficulty that other children his or her age have used for years, the student may have difficulty controlling the anger and frustration that accompanies his or her struggle in math. The student's lack of ability to regulate emotions might make him or her seem immature for a middle school student. However, if the student has not had to exercise coping and regulatory skills, this will be new learning for the student. In both examples, students' cognitive, physical, and emotional development are out of sync. This asynchrony is typical in gifted students, and may many times be the root of social-emotional issues you notice in the classroom.

Being aware that your students' cognitive, social-emotional, and physical development may be asynchronous helps you keep your teacher expectations in check. For example, you may regularly teach your third-grade class at a Lexile, content, and "big idea" level more commensurate with fifth grade, but then be surprised when a student in this classroom who is so academically capable has a meltdown because he or she cannot resolve a conflict with a peer. Or your class may spend weeks on a multipart project, complete with rich discussions, well thought-out rubrics, and lots of opportunities for creative and abstract thinking. However, when students present final products, you are all a little disappointed in the quality. In situations like these, remind yourself that the students are still 9. Yes, they have the capacity to think and reason in a way that is well beyond their years, but at the end of the day they still need the same types of scaffolded expectations as other children.

When you understand and expect your students to be out of sync, you can anticipate certain SEL opportunities and teaching points. Identifying resources and strategies for self-regulation is definitely a practice in which you will want to invest some time. High intellect or academic ability does not equal advanced-level self-awareness or regulatory ability. These skills need to be explicitly taught. When one's body or emotions cannot keep up with the brain, knowing how and when to defuse will equip students with the tools to stay engaged and regulated. Ask yourself, "Is my student upset/disengaged/anxious/stressed because there is a mismatch between the activity or situation and his or her abilities?" This type of questioning is a great first step to being aware of how issues associated with asynchronous development can manifest in your classroom.

CHALLENGE AND FAILURE

All students respond differently to academic challenges and failure. Gifted students, when experiencing these feelings for the first time, may need additional support in coping with and overcoming their difficulties for a number of reasons. In a study of gifted students' implicit beliefs about intelligence and giftedness, Makel, Snyder, Thomas, Malone, and Putallaz (2015) found that many students believed intelligence was flexible, but giftedness was fixed. With this mindset, it is no wonder that when something is too hard or when students fail, they feel that it is a threat to their giftedness. If your students believe that giftedness is an integral part of who they are as people, rather than a characteristic of how they learn, it would be difficult to come to terms with struggling and failure. This not only impacts students' self-efficacy, but also can cause anxiety surrounding academic achievement, which can have long-term negative repercussions.

In your classroom, work to normalize failure and conscientiously point out how challenges require new ways of thinking or approaching a topic. Teach students that failure is not a sign of weakness, but a tool with which they can learn and build new skills and abilities (Salmela & Määttä, 2015). Also talk openly with your students about giftedness. One's academic strengths and talents don't define a person or give him or her worth; instead, understanding one's areas of giftedness helps students and teachers to understand what each individual needs in order to learn and grow. Students are not the sum of their achievements, nor does failure does not take away from who they are as people. You can reinforce this idea through several classroom practices and structures. Consider implementing a workshop model during at least part of your instructional time, so that

> LEAD BY EXAMPLE: MAKE VISIBLE MISTAKES, MODEL HOW TO CORRECT THEM, AND MOVE ON.

students can have an opportunity for intervention (i.e., "teacher table time") as needed. Working through difficult material in a smaller group with other students who need additional support opens up a safe environment for struggle.

You can also lead by example: Make visible mistakes, model how to correct them, and move on. Think out loud the problem-solving process for fixing mistakes, and connect the ways in which failing in the moment will help one be successful in the long term. For example, do a math problem incorrectly and, when the missteps are inevitably pointed out, explain how such an error is easy to make. When you model writing for your students, use words you are not sure how to spell and cross out ideas you decide not to include. If you are working on a prototype for a hands-on activity, engineer a part poorly so that you can model the redesign and revision process. Obviously, you want to practice making mistakes during the practice portion of the lesson cycle, and not when delivering brand-new information. When you are introducing new concepts, acknowledge that the more complex parts may be challenging to conceptualize and understand at first, and reiterate that students do not have to be experts right then. Reinforce the ongoing nature of knowledge-building. Create a gifted classroom in which healthy mistakes and failure are expected, because these are opportunities to learn. Remind students that if they are not successful today, it does not mean they will not be tomorrow, and that failure does not change the intrinsic makeup of who they are as individuals.

PeRFecTIonISM

Perfectionism is a personality trait developed over time (Rule & Montgomery, 2013) that is "characterized by striving for flawlessness and setting excessively high standards for performance accompanied by overly critical evaluations of one's behavior" (as cited in Smith, Saklofske, Stoeber, & Sherry, 2016, p. 670). Smith et al. (2016) outlined 10 facets of perfectionism, which include self-oriented perfectionism, self-worth contingencies, concern over mistakes, doubts across actions, self-criticism, socially pre-scribed perfectionism, other-oriented perfectionism, hypercriti-cism, grandiosity, and entitlement. Clearly, perfectionism can stem from a number of beliefs and experiences processed by students over time. Although they may not realize it, educators and par-ents may support adaptive perfectionism by reinforcing some per-fectionist behaviors, such as working hard and setting lofty goals (Rule & Montgomery, 2013). But that is what educators want all children to do—work hard and set high goals—right? How can educators encourage high achievement while avoiding encourag-ing the internalization of negative perfectionist traits?

The road to developing academic tenacity and ambitious goal-setting, but avoiding the pitfalls associated with perfection-ism, is one that educators should tread carefully with gifted stu-dents. When challenges and failures, as discussed in the previous section, become points that make or break students, you should examine the situation to determine whether perfectionistic behav-iors and beliefs are negatively impacting your students' ability to learn and grow. Perfectionism can manifest in several different ways, such as through:

- dichotomous thinking (i.e., "all or nothing") telling an individual that anything less than perfection is failure,
- underachievement ("If I can't do it perfectly, I won't try to do it at all."),
- avoidance ("If I put it off and run out of time, at least I didn't fail."),
- the belief that social acceptance depends on perfect performance,
- lack of pride in one's work (Rule & Montgomery, 2013),
- setting unrealistically high standards, and
- assuming that failure in one area means one cannot be successful in any area or venture (McGee & Hughes, 2011).

Do any of these perfectionist tendencies look familiar? You may even notice a few in yourself or others you know. Understanding how we can avoid exacerbating perfectionistic ideas and attitudes can help our students reverse some perfectionist behaviors that are hindering their achievement, happiness, and positive self-efficacy.

You can work to curb perfectionist attitudes and behaviors in many different ways. Provide students with ongoing feedback, rather than waiting until the end of an activity, project, or assignment. Students with perfectionistic tendencies will fixate on your final appraisal of their work and minimize or ignore the actual learning process required to generate that product. Feedback should be more reflective in nature, rather than strictly evaluative. This shift can be as simple as changing a statement to a question.

> **FEEDBACK THAT IS ONGOING AND FOCUSED ON THE LEARNING, INSTEAD OF A FINAL PRODUCT, WILL HELP REDIRECT STUDENTS' FOCUS FROM AN ALL-OR-NOTHING END GOAL MENTALITY.**

For example, if a student is building a rocket, instead of saying, "That fin shape will not work well if you want your rocket to fly far," simply ask, "Can you tell me a little more about why you shaped the fin the way you did?" Not only will you get students to stretch the metacognitive muscles to explain their thinking, but also you will give them a chance to catch their own mistakes in a much lower risk situation than testing the rocket in front of the whole class.

Your feedback should also praise the process, rather than the product (Rule & Montgomery, 2013). You can tell students things like, "I love how hard you're thinking about the fin shape. Remember, we're engineers, so if this version doesn't work like you wanted, you can always redesign and retry." Feedback that is ongoing and focused on the learning, instead of a final product, will help redirect students' focus from an all-or-nothing end goal mentality.

Setting a series of smaller, more attainable goals is another way to minimize perfectionist thinking (Rule & Montgomery, 2013). A small series of goals, which one can complete without necessarily doing each at 100%, that add up to one large accomplishment also helps students to shift their thinking toward a process orientation. If there are a series of steps, this minimizes the opportunity to believe that a task is either perfectly executed or a complete loss, because there is a "next." Setting and reflecting on goals along the way also helps students see that even if some small thing is not done perfectly, the final product can still be high quality and worthwhile. Breaking things down into a series of steps or goals also supports those students who have difficulty beginning or completing something for fear of failure. A clear direction and goal, with many checkpoints along the way, helps provide students with a pathway of continued support.

Combating perfectionism is an ongoing process, and this type of thinking will not be removed from your students overnight. Working to help students overcome perfectionist attitudes and behaviors may even take years. Begin by creating a classroom that welcomes open discussion of challenge and its associated frustrations. Let students know that you expect and embrace failure, and this can help make a shift in perfectionistic thinking. Establishing learning, not final products, as the ultimate goal, setting up a reasonable series of steps to reach that goal, and providing ongoing feedback create an environment that helps students combat perfectionism. Although this will not eliminate all perfectionistic thoughts and behaviors in your students, these practices and structures seek to minimize the attitudes and actions that perpetuate perfectionist thinking.

MOTIVATION AND ACHIEVEMENT

Student motivation and achievement are closely linked to the topics already discussed in this chapter: self-efficacy beliefs, mindset about challenges and failure, and perfectionism. Many times, student achievement (or lack thereof) is where teachers first get clued in to these other issues. When gifted students are not realizing their potential or making expected academic gains in terms of talent development, that is frequently the impetus for parents and teachers to dig for underlying issues. When students underachieve, there is an observable discrepancy between expected and actual performance (Siegle, 2013). Gifted students are at risk for underachievement, potentially due to motivation (Reis & Renzulli, 2009) that has waned due to beliefs about self, school, and perfectionist thinking. Teachers need the tools to identify the motivational factors and their underlying causes that can hold students back.

Students who have high self-concepts of ability and high levels of self-efficacy typically also demonstrate motivational behavior that contributes to task orientation and performance, although there are certainly other personal and contextual factors that can influence achievement (Dai, Moon, & Feldhusen, 1998). Supporting students who struggle with establishing realistic beliefs about achievement, giving specific and targeted feedback ("When you solved that problem, going back to your notes to find the best strategy really helped," versus, "Good job solving that problem"), and modeling for students how to accurately attribute success are all strategies for increasing self-concept and self-efficacy. The ways in which we give feedback need to encourage students to believe that they possess the skills necessary for success. What you tell your students should not only recognize their talent, but also attribute its development to the student (Siegle & McCoach, 2005). These beliefs about self have the potential to positively or negatively influence motivation.

You are likely familiar with the constructs of extrinsic and intrinsic motivation and the impact of motivation on student learning and achievement. Students who lack motivation are likely underachieving, and students who feel too much motivation to achieve may take on perfectionistic tendencies. Helpful suggestions for supporting healthy motivation were assembled by Siegle and McCoach (2005) in their work on motivating underachieving gifted students. One of the key aspects of engaging students is painting a clear picture of why they are learning or studying a topic. Why is it important today, and how will it impact the future? Simply connecting the learning objectives with an overall wider purpose will help even very young students understand why it is important to engage with the content. If you cannot answer that "why" question regarding the learning, consider how your students must feel. Superfluous or flashy activities that do not connect to broader topics will likely not motivate students (see Chapter 1). Illustrating to students the rationale and larger-scale connections involved in learning is essential in sustaining both extrinsic and intrinsic motivation.

Students who are appropriately challenged demonstrate motivated learner behaviors, which is why it is so important for gifted students to have the opportunity to work with like-ability peers (Kitsantas, Bland, & Chirinos, 2017). When students can work at a level of cognitive demand with other like-ability students who can provide feedback and support, engagement and interest replace unmotivated, "checked out" behaviors. If students perceive school as a place that is boring, that may be because they do not have enough opportunities to work with other kids who challenge them. If the teacher is the only person in the room who can cognitively challenge a student, that student will quickly lose motivation to engage and participate. Although children should develop skills for collaboration with a variety of other learners, equally important is that they work with peers who think and process in the same advanced ways that they do. Make sure your grouping strategies, or those strategies you coach classroom teachers on, include ample opportunity for students to work with others who have similar skills and abilities.

You can also build and sustain motivation in your students by helping them set goals, providing ongoing feedback, and reflecting on progress (Siegle & McCoach, 2005). These same strategies to address perfectionism can also help get students out of the under-achievement rut through giving them attainable steps that feel good to accomplish. When students receive consistent encouragement and have chances to reflect on their own talent development, they see a bigger-picture view of how their actions result in positive growth. Students who can look at their work and see a definite trend in improvement, complexity, or quality will be more likely to persevere forward.

Motivation is influenced by both personal and environmental factors (Clinkenbeard, 2012). You can structure your classroom in such a way that students have the opportunity to work both independently and in flexible groups, and build choice into the types of activities offered. You may hook students' interest in the classroom and boost intrinsic motivation through learning what their interests are outside of the classroom (Clinkenbeard, 2012). Allow students to pursue those interests independently or in tandem with the gifted curriculum (Siegle & McCoach, 2005). Provide goal-setting structures and consistent affirmations, along with the opportunity to engage in authentic learning with real, observable outcomes, and this will help boost your students' motivation to achieve and take ownership of learning.

> WHEN STUDENTS RECEIVE CONSISTENT ENCOURAGEMENT AND HAVE CHANCES TO REFLECT ON THEIR OWN TALENT DEVELOPMENT, THEY SEE A BIGGER-PICTURE VIEW OF HOW THEIR ACTIONS RESULT IN POSITIVE GROWTH.

CAMPUSWIDE SOCIAL-EMOTIONAL SUPPORT

The gifted teacher cannot be the only social and emotional support for students. As with all kids, a team of people working together is necessary to make sure their needs are met and they are growing as both scholars and individuals. In addition to the other classroom teachers, a great resource to tap into is your school counselor. The American School Counselor Association (ASCA, 2017) formally recognized that the counselor:

> delivers a comprehensive school counseling program to meet students' academic, career and social/emotional needs. Gifted and talented students have unique and diverse developmental needs that are addressed by school counselors . . . in collaboration with other educators and stakeholders. (p. 35)

However, you may need to work on actively connecting students who need counseling support with the counselors because unless these students are experiencing academic challenges, gifted students may be overlooked (Kennedy & Farley, 2018). When a gifted student suffers academically, alarm bells go off. But giftedness and high achievement can mask other underlying issues, and students can fly undetected under the counselor's radar. Keep the lines of communication with your school counselor clear, and make sure that parents and students know that the counselor is a resource for support for their students' social-emotional needs, too.

The students' other teachers are also good resources for insight into the social-emotional well-being of kids. If teachers report unmotivated or underachieving students, remind them of the effective grouping practices that will allow gifted students to work with like-ability peers in their classrooms, and make sure this is happening with regularity. You could also partner with those teachers to provide independent learning contracts or interest-related extensions that appeal to the students. Being aware of significantly "off" behavior in certain classes can help you act as an advocate for your students. The classroom teachers are additional sets of eyes and ears to help watch out for any social-emotional issues that might arise.

Communicating with other classroom teachers may also reveal some unrealistic teacher ideas about or expectations for gifted students. Sometimes, teachers will hold gifted students to higher standards than others. This can lead to unnecessary stress and anxiety for students, as well as an imbalance of schoolwork and opportunities for them to pursue interests outside of school (Kitsantas et al., 2017), not to mention the tension it creates between the gifted students and the others in the classroom. Talking to other teachers can give you a big-picture view of students' behaviors and perceived needs in other classes, which is helpful in targeting and identifying specific variables that affect attitudes and behaviors.

Engaging campuswide social-emotional support for gifted students is also important because studies show that frequently gifted students experienced difficulties with peer relationships (McGee & Hughes, 2011; Salmela & Määttä, 2015). Issues associated with asynchronous development, difficulties navigating between academic and social situations, and just the process of building an identity as a child and young adult can be a source of conflict between gifted and other students. Creating the awareness that this is an issue of which all faculty can be mindful will help widen the scope of support gifted students receive at school. If other adults, such as coaches, administrators, counselors, and aides, can anticipate difficulties in peer relations, they can take steps to give students situation-specific (i.e., in athletics, in nonacademic classes, during lunch and recess) tools to help navigate relationships that can be hard at times. A campuswide awareness of how and why gifted students may have difficulty navigating peer relationships at times widens the net of social-emotional support far outside the walls of the gifted classroom.

Building campuswide support also helps you do more for your students through building capacity in others. In a study by Wood (2010), gifted students were asked to select opportunities that they believed would help support their academic success, and many of their responses included social-emotional components.

Respondents said that the following opportunities would be beneficial:

- meeting adults who had careers in their field of interest,
- chances to work with other students who had similar interests,
- having an avenue to discuss class structures and challenge level that they liked or disliked,
- making "academic blueprints" or outlines for current and future plans, and
- support with time management and organization.

This is certainly a tall order, but something your gifted students need and deserve. Opportunities like these help increase and sustain motivation and achievement, and give students ownership of their academic development. It is not possible for you to provide students with this type of support all on your own, so reaching out to the larger school community is essential. As with everything else discussed in this book, start small. Facilitate a team of a few key supports, use that momentum to inform and include others, and work to build capacity over time. Meeting students' social and emotional needs is complex and can oftentimes seem a little muddy. Having a group of people with whom you can reflect, rethink, and strategize is key in being the most effective social-emotional support you can be.

CHAPTER 6
SPECIAL POPULATIONS

Student body populations are becoming increasingly diverse, with schools providing more support services for special education and traditionally underserved groups of students. Reflective of the identification, monitoring, and support of these students on our campuses, educators should also see an increase in students with diverse needs and backgrounds in gifted classrooms. However, this change has been slow to come. Students with special needs and who are twice-exceptional and students from culturally, linguistically, and economically diverse (CLED) backgrounds have not appeared in gifted classrooms as quickly as educators have been able to identify them in the general student population. Deficit views of students with special education needs or limited knowledge of 2e as a construct (Foley-Nicpon, Assouline, & Colangelo, 2013) may keep them from being referred for gifted services. Students from low-income and minority backgrounds are less likely to be identified as gifted (Woods, 2016). As a gifted teacher, your role in supporting schoolwide awareness of the potential in these students is critical. Learning how to advocate for mindsets and practices that are inclusive of all students when it comes to gifted services will help to improve equity in opportunities for all.

Understanding the ways in which you can support identification of these students and how you can adapt the subsequent services they receive in order to develop their unique skills and talents is so important. As you make progress in utilizing more equitable identification practices, you will see an increasing number of students with diverse backgrounds and abilities in your classroom. Anticipating and preparing for the needs of these students will help you create an environment that is welcoming and inclusive, and optimal for learning.

TWICE-EXCEPTIONAL STUDENTS

The Twice-Exceptional Community of Practice (2e CoP) created this definition statement to outline the characteristics and needs of 2e students:

> Twice exceptional (2e) individuals evidence exceptional ability and disability, which results in a unique set of circumstances. Their exceptional ability may dominate, hiding their disability; their disability may dominate, hiding their exceptional ability; each may mask the other so that neither is recognized or addressed.
>
> 2e students, who may perform below, at or above grade level, require the following:
> » Specialized methods of identification that consider the possible interaction of the exceptionalities.
> » Enriched/advanced educational opportunities that develop the child's interests, gifts and talents while also meeting the child's learning needs.
> » Simultaneous supports that ensure the child's academic success and social-emotional well-being, such as accommodations, therapeutic interventions, and specialized instruction.

Recall the construct of asynchronous development we discussed in Chapter 5. Twice-exceptional students exhibit asynchronous learning needs, due to their complex and varied academic strengths and areas requiring intervention or accommodation (Coleman & Gallagher, 2015). Comparing these constructs is helpful in framing your understanding of the ways in which gifts and disabilities can converge and affect students. You may know that, as an example of asynchronous development, students' hands might not be able to keep up with their heads in expressing ideas, due to a discrepancy between cognitive processing and motor skills. You may also know that a student may communicate with you like an adult in terms of language and ideas, but then have an emotional meltdown because he or she struggles to develop appropriate social and emotional regulatory skills. Twice-exceptional students have similar out-of-sync needs as far as academics and learning. A student with dyslexia may struggle to read words on a page and be a brilliant mathematician. A student with an attention disorder may be a gifted writer.

But where is teachers' natural inclination to focus? Certainly on the areas where students need extra support, because that is what teachers have been trained to do—help students succeed through building knowledge and closing gaps. Educators either do not look for or do not know that these students, who may experience academic struggles due to a disability, also can possess immense potential for advanced talent development. Viewing students through the lens of what they cannot do is an example of deficit thinking, as is allowing what students struggle with to define how you see them as learners. Understanding that both giftedness and learning needs that require special education services can exist in the same student helps us avoid this type of deficit thinking and be more open to the dual but equal nature of our students' needs.

CHARACTERISTICS OF TWICE-EXCEPTIONAL STUDENTS

Students with learning disorders, Attention Deficit/Hyperactivity Disorder (ADHD), autism spectrum disorders (ASD;

Assouline & Whiteman, 2011), and physical impairments are all included under the 2e umbrella. Although this is not an exhaustive list of the types of special needs 2e students may have, it does provide you with some of the most common examples of twice-exceptionalities seen in our classrooms. Many times, we do not realize that these students receiving special education supports also possess gifted levels of potential. Gifted students with special education needs can easily go unidentified because their strengths and disabilities can cancel one another out (Amend & Peters, 2015). A student could appear average because there is no readily identifiable deficiency not explained by a disability, nor is there any evident outstanding area of potential. For instance, a student with ADHD may seem like an average learner who is able to manage an attention disorder with relative success. In reality, this student is using all of his or her cognitive skills to manage behavior, so the student doesn't have the opportunity to show what his or her true academic abilities are without expending considerable energy on impulse control. When identifying potential 2e students, ask yourself if there are ways to look for giftedness that allow the student to let go of compensatory behaviors and allow his or her true abilities to become evident.

> **VIEWING STUDENTS THROUGH THE LENS OF WHAT THEY CANNOT DO IS AN EXAMPLE OF DEFICIT THINKING, AS IS ALLOWING WHAT STUDENTS STRUGGLE WITH TO DEFINE HOW YOU SEE THEM AS LEARNERS.**

Twice-exceptional students can engage in both conscious and unconscious compensation; that is, one part of the brain or body, or a specific behavior, may take over to make up for deficiencies in other areas (Silverman, 2009). Because a disability can mask traits of giftedness, students may be identified as either gifted or as needing special education services, but not both. In order to identify potential 2e students, teachers and other adults must pay close attention to behaviors specific to academic learning, whether students rely on one tried-and-true strategy to get them through school, and how they perform when they are given a variety of options to demonstrate mastery. Can they switch, with relative ease, from one way of learning or engaging with the material to the other? Do they seem disengaged because they are using all of their energy to not blurt out, move too much, and get in trouble? Are their physical needs limiting the ways in which they can respond and demonstrate their areas of strength? These are the types of important questions to ask of our students if we suspect that there may be other underlying issues affecting their performance and behavior in school.

Identification, using standard assessment tools, may be difficult for 2e students. Depending on the type of tests used, a student's scores may be all over the map. Significant discrepancies in test scores can point to the possibility of two exceptionalities in students who appear average (Amend & Peters, 2015), and they can also illustrate the areas in which a student's disability might be hindering gifted levels of performance in other areas. When assessing a student with special education needs for gifted services, point out any discrepancies in quantitative data and ask what they could mean, in terms of masking a strength. In your qualitative data, you may consider including classroom observations or interviews that you do with the student, performance-based tasks, and feedback from the special education teachers. Although it is not advisable to completely disregard the formal testing process for identification, be creative and include examples, like the ones listed here, in your overall assessment of the student. Also, certainly structure testing environments in a way that helps minimize a negative influence of any disabilities (this is outlined in the student's IEP or 504 paperwork) so that the quantitative assessments you administer give the best reflection of the student's true skills. Do not be surprised if data on 2e students have discrepancies. Use these clues to help fit together a larger, more complete picture of a student's academic ability.

In the classroom, 2e students may demonstrate a variety of behaviors and traits. Problems with short-term memory, preference for spatial tasks, verbal precocity but poor reading, restlessness/fidgeting, being easily distracted, difficulty understanding social contexts, impulsivity, emotional volatility, and difficulty following directions and finishing tasks are all commonly observed (Reis, Baum, & Burke, 2014). Although some of these can definitely present challenges for teachers, remember that these are symptoms or manifestations of a student's disability. Following the same accommodations, modifications, and behavior redirection strategies as the general education classroom teachers is key in establishing consistency and predictability, which students need. Going back to the idea that academic intelligence does not equal emotional, behavioral, or social ability, remember to build in teaching time for establishing rules and procedures.

Twice-exceptional students may need more explicit teaching or practice to be successful, and this is perfectly acceptable. Strategies like chunking activities and assignments, providing frequent breaks, using nonverbal cues, and giving students who are upset a space to de-escalate safely can all be implemented fairly easily in the course of your regular instruction. Do not be afraid to ask for in-class support or specific strategies from the special education department if needed, either. The goal is to provide continuous, academically appropriate services to students, and you may need help reaching this goal sometimes. Knowing the students' backgrounds, specific behaviors and needs, being able to anticipate where they will need additional support, and having effective strategies in place that are consistent across classrooms will help you in designing a classroom environment that encourages and grows all learners equitably.

STRENGTHS-BASED APPROACHES

As stated previously, deficit thinking, or basing one's beliefs and assumptions around students based on what they can't do, colors teachers' view of 2e students. When you start looking at what students can do, and how you can leverage these strengths and interests in order to help support learning, you are taking a strengths-based approach to gifted education. Coleman and Gallagher (2015) called for "multidimensional supports and services" for students that help to develop talents through engaging student strengths and providing appropriate accommodations or modifications when needed. This does not mean that you lessen the challenge or lower your expectations; the rigor of the content should be appropriate for the students' cognitive level, and the students should share an environment of high expectations. The way in which they interact with that rigorous content should not be hampered by their disability, and students should have opportunities that allow them to demonstrate mastery through their academic areas of strength.

When students can experience growth and success in an environment that focuses on their abilities, 2e students will build high academic self-concept and self-efficacy (Wang & Neihart, 2015). Strategies that encourage a strengths-based approach to learning and instruction include greater choice and flexibility in topics studied, and the method of learning, pacing that is responsive to student needs, opportunities for collaboration (Willard-Holt, Weber, Morrison, & Horgan, 2013), providing positive peer influences to foster positive self-efficacy, and ongoing parent and teacher support (Wang & Neihart, 2015). Taking a strengths-based approach to instruction when working with 2e students allows everyone— teachers, parents, and the students themselves—to really see children's talents developed and harnessed for creative productivity and problem solving (Omdal, 2015). You owe it to your students to see them in their entirety, not just through a deficit lens.

CULTURALLY, LINGUISTICALLY, AND ECONOMICALLY DIVERSE STUDENTS

Culturally, linguistically, and economically diverse gifted students are children whose race, ethnicity, cultural practices, and socioeconomic status do not fit the affluent, Anglo-oriented, stereotypical view of what a typical gifted student looks like. Although these factors, in a perfect world, should not keep a student from being identified as gifted, socioeconomic status and race can actually better predict whether a student is identified as gifted than academic factors (Sullivan, 2011). This text has discussed strategies for building equity into identification practices, but this is a much larger, ongoing advocacy conversation in which scholars and practitioners will continue to engage.

Your role as a gifted teacher is to support these equitable practices on your campus. Be mindful that the population of your gifted classroom should look very much like the overall population of your school, and if it does not, start asking whether all students are on equal footing in your current identification practices. If your classroom is full of White and Asian students when your school is predominantly Black and Hispanic, there's a problem, and it's time to start brainstorming solutions with your leadership team. If your demographics are changing, it's time to start asking how identification practices will change to accommodate your increasingly diverse student body. You may have limited capacity to actually implement these changes (or it may be entirely up to you—this is dependent on the additional responsibilities associated with being a gifted teacher), but you can be a vocal support and advocate for equity in identification.

In a study by Briggs, Reis, and Sullivan (2008), researchers identified some key points that contributed to successful identification and inclusion of CLED students in gifted services. Schools cast a wider net to identify these students when they modify the procedures used. Alternative assessment strategies, such as the use of performance-based tasks, portfolios, and nonverbal assessments, increase students' opportunities to demonstrate giftedness. Most teachers understand that CLED students express their abilities in different ways than their White, English-speaking peers. Moreover, standardized assessments or traditional metrics like IQ scores may not paint an accurate picture of these students' abilities (de Wet & Gubbins, 2011). Including a variety of assessment options allows you to be flexible and responsive when it comes to identifying giftedness in diverse student populations. In selecting equitable identification resources, remember that your measures should match the services provided. Any alternative assessments you select should be used in tandem with other data and parent/teacher feedback to paint the most holistic picture of the student as possible, in order to most accurately identify an appropriate academic fit for gifted services.

Schools can also identify students with high potential and then even the playing field before assessment through front-loading opportunities. Students from low-income backgrounds may not have the same early childhood opportunities as their peers. These students may have had little or no academic support (reading with parents, early childhood learning programs, etc.) prior to kindergarten, so they begin their school career at a considerable disadvantage. This does not mean that they do not have high potential. When you start a race a mile behind, it is hard to catch up with everyone else, let alone win. If students have the chance to interact with high-level content prior to formal identification, they are afforded an additional opportunity to catch up (Briggs, Reis, & Sullivan, 2008). The front-loaded access to higher level thinking provides students a bridge (Stambaugh, 2010) to the thinking and processing skills that their home or early childhood environment may not have provided. In utilizing this strategy, you are not giving students an unfair advantage; you are eliminating an unfair disadvantage. It is not an equitable practice to test students on skills they have not had sufficient opportunity to process and practice. This two-stage practice of identifying high potential, and then providing scaffolded learning experiences prior to assessment is an effective strategy that can provide a clearer picture of how students may develop their talents as a result of gifted programming intervention.

Once students are identified, gifted services should be structured in such a way that allows CLED students to experience

> **YOU CAN BE A VOCAL SUPPORT AND ADVOCATE FOR EQUITY IN IDENTIFICATION.**

academic success (Briggs, Reis, & Sullivan, 2008). Selecting curriculum materials that make authentic, real-world connections to these students' world is critical in engaging these students in learning (Stambaugh, 2010). Remember the principles for selecting appropriate curriculum that we discussed in Chapter 1? Revisit principles 3–5 (Hockett, 2009):

- Principle 3: Curriculum engages students in thinking like disciplinarians.
- Principle 4: Curriculum emphasizes authentic, real-world problems, products, and performances.
- Principle 5: Curriculum is flexible in pacing and variety, and structured so that students can engage in self-directed learning and the pursuit of individual interests.

Consider this example: High-quality curriculum that compares and analyzes canonical British literature and connects it to the social and political injustices of today meets these principles, but it would likely not be relevant to the worlds of your CLED students. This content would need to be modified to include writers and famous figures from students' cultures and backgrounds. The social and political injustices should be specific to your community, so that you can then scaffold the content to include a more global view. As your classroom becomes more diverse, you should modify the curriculum content to reflect the backgrounds, experiences, and worlds of your students. This makes the learning more interesting and accessible and shows your students that you see them. If you are to develop the potential of gifted CLED students, it is also necessary to modify or develop curriculum (Tomlinson & Jarvis, 2014) to make it relatable, accessible, and communicate high expectations that are respectful of students' backgrounds.

Is working toward equity in identification and service for CLED students a challenge? Absolutely. Sometimes you will not know what you do not know, and learning takes time. You may have to try a number of strategies and approaches before one sticks, and this can be a frustrating process. But there is good news: "Teachers and schools can positively affect achievement without being exemplary in all facets of their practice" (Tomlinson

& Jarvis, 2014, p. 191). This finding comes from case studies of CLED gifted students, and it gives hope when making major changes might seem impossible. You do not have to be perfect, but you do have to try. Programmatic transformation does not happen overnight. Be thoughtful and deliberate when evaluating your program's current state and identify possible solutions that will work in the context of your school. Develop a plan and seek out support. As an advocate for your students and as a leader in your program, you need to set measurable goals, involve other teachers and campus leadership in implementing these goals, and engage in purposeful evaluation practices that highlight CLED student success (Briggs, Reis, & Sullivan, 2008; Swanson, 2016). Identify ways in which you can make your program more inclusive, involve others in meeting this goal, and use student outcomes as your markers for success. This is what will help drive changes that make a big impact in the present and in years to come.

Inclusivity and equity in gifted services can have a significant schoolwide impact. If students are unidentified, they are likely underperforming in their current academic placement. Opportunities to uncover and develop potential can transform these learners into high achievers, creative producers, and innovative problem solvers. Imagine how this could change your campus culture, attitudes and beliefs about giftedness, and overall transformation in teaching and learning (Swanson, 2016). These rewards are certainly worth the leadership efforts necessary to make changes.

SPECIAL POPULATIONS IN GIFTED EDUCATION

As a field, gifted education continues to work toward equity and inclusivity for all students. Gifted education must separate itself from its elitist reputation and truly be accessible for all students who need advanced, accelerated, and complex instruction in order to maximize their potential. Being aware of how all-encompassing gifted services should be and including students from traditionally underrepresented and underserved groups may mean changing what teachers think about their students, the capacity to learn, and ways to identify and develop potential. However difficult this seems, remember that the direct results of championing these students are increased achievement, more creative problem solvers, and more students who are tuned in to school because they own and value the learning.

CHAPTER 7

ONGOING PROFESSIONAL LEARNING

As you reflect on your initial experiences in teaching gifted or anticipate the changes your new assignment will bring in the coming year, you may feel overwhelmed with questions or uncertainties about next steps in growing your craft. By engaging in a variety of professional learning experiences, you can start piecing together the answers to your questions, resources and strategies for effective instruction, and the security of knowing that you have the skills and knowledge to be a successful gifted teacher. Quality professional development and learning experiences keep educators "fresh"—effective teacher training equips teachers with research-supported best practices and knowledge to continually improve their teaching. Professional learning helps build awareness of the changes and trends in the field and helps anticipate future areas for growth. The importance of meaningful, targeted professional learning cannot be understated.

If you have not experienced such fulfilling, robust professional learning that has shaped you into a capable professional in the field of gifted education, you are in good company. The fact is, even if you went through a university teacher-training program during your time as an undergraduate student, gifted education is typically offered beginning at the graduate level (Reis & Westberg, 1994). So you likely got little to no exposure to the field of gifted education during your own academic career unless you sought out additional courses. As a teacher, you may not have experienced too much transformative gifted professional learning through your school, either. Westberg et al. (1998) found that very little of a school district's professional learning budget is allocated for gifted-specific topics, gifted specialists infrequently provide professional learning for teachers, most districts do not evaluate the specific impact of professional learning on gifted education, and ongoing opportunities for collaboration and coaching between the gifted and general education teachers are "seldom to never" used as a form of professional learning. Additionally, professional learning opportunities may be limited in your area, or you simply may not know where to look for quality training and instruction for teachers of gifted students. Quality professional learning for gifted teachers can be difficult to find. This chapter discusses professional learning expectations, strategies, and resources that can help keep you learning and growing in the field of gifted education.

PROFESSIONAL LEARNING EXPECTATIONS

As part of becoming a gifted teacher, you may have had to complete specific professional learning trainings, passed a certification test, or fulfilled other specific teaching proficiencies. For example, in Texas, teachers of gifted students must complete 30 hours of articulated gifted professional development sessions prior to actually teaching gifted classes, then complete an annual 6-hour update (Texas Education Agency, 2019). This requirement is outlined in the Texas State Plan for the Education of Gifted/Talented Students. Gifted teacher training and qualification criteria vary from state to state, so you should familiarize yourself with your state's expectations, organizations, and resources. Your state may have an organization that provides professional development opportunities and guidance in interpreting and implementing education code regarding gifted programming. Nationwide, gifted teachers, students, and parents have NAGC, an organization made up of practitioners, scholars, researchers, and other stakeholders in the field. NAGC, in coordination with The Association for the Gifted, Council for Exceptional Children (CEC-TAG), set nationally-recognized programming standards for gifted services. These programming standards are broken up into different categories, and Standard 6 is where you find information regarding professional development. According to these standards, gifted teachers should be able to use professional ethical principles and standards-based programming practices; have a foundational knowledge of the perspectives, history, and current issues and events in gifted education; understand and model respect for diversity in gifted education; be an active participant in professional learning; and work to advance the profession through direct advocacy for and involvement with students (NAGC & CEC-TAG, 2013). Familiarizing yourself with these national expectations for professional development is a great place to start in understanding what types of opportunities to seek out.

NAGC is an organization that provides guidance, a community of gifted advocates, and resources for teachers. Your state and local policies, however, may vary. Gifted education programs are the responsibility of the state and school district. In terms of national laws, there are currently no specific mandates that outline provisions for gifted education (Shaunessey, 2003). Your state's education website is a great place to begin in understanding exactly what the expectations for gifted teachers and gifted programming are. Use these expectations, along with those outlined by NAGC and CEC-TAG (2013), to form a baseline for the types of professional learning to seek out. A plan for your professional learning and development that is standards-based will allow you to evaluate how the professional learning affects your teaching, how it affects the ways in which pedagogy and content knowledge come together, and how it grows your professional knowledge (Johnsen & Clarenbach, 2017).

SELECTING PROFESSIONAL LEARNING

Quality training and the time in which one can engage in professional learning are two major challenges when discussing professional growth (Young & Balli, 2014). You may be used to getting suggestions or options for useful, targeted training from your campus leadership team. Perhaps you are used to selecting professional development based on the feedback from your administrators. Being a gifted teacher is a little different in this respect. Typically, tools for teacher evaluation and feedback do not include components specific to gifted education (Johnsen, 2013), so many times your feedback is not specific to the nature and needs of the gifted classroom. How, then, do you know where you need to go, or the learning needed to get there?

> **THE GOAL OF PROFESSIONAL LEARNING IS DEVELOPING STUDENT TALENT.**

Begin with the standards, whether they are from your state, NACG, or both. Notice that the goal of professional learning is developing student talent. When selecting professional learning, ask yourself whether the goals and objectives listed in the description will help you to make the choices and adaptations to instructions that will result in a positive change in your students' learning (Dai & Chen, 2013). If the professional learning focuses heavily on one-shot types of activities, ask yourself whether this learning can be generalized into a variety of teaching and learning applications (Garet et al., 2001). If you can only see using the strategies that you learned in isolated situations, then that particular offering might not be the best use of your valuable time.

Who is leading the learning? The facilitator should have recent, practical experience with what he or she is teaching (Wycoff, Nash, Juntune, & Mackay, 2003). If this is a professional learning opportunity that is offered by the same facilitator, year after year, you have to wonder how fresh and relevant the content can be. Offering the same high-quality content regularly so that teachers have ample opportunity to benefit is certainly possible, but if the material isn't updated or doesn't evolve with new applications or examples, then you may find that it's not particularly relevant. The facilitator should also be able to speak to the common stumbling blocks associated with the content, provide real-world examples of successful and unsuccessful implementation, and be able to link the material with up-to-date research and knowledge.

What are the key takeaways from the professional learning? Is the main takeaway a big, nebulous concept with few actionable strategies? That might be appropriate if you are building foundational knowledge of a foreign topic. If you are looking for learning that is implementable in the classroom, this probably is not the best choice. Select professional learning that outlines specific content-based knowledge and provides strategies for implementation (DeMonte, 2013; Garet et al., 2001).

Closely examine the format of the professional learning. Will it mostly involve sit-and-get lecture? If the learning does not involve opportunities for you to try the strategy (DeMonte, 2013; Garet et al., 2001), ask yourself how likely you will actually be to implement what you learned in the classroom. You would not expect your students to perform a new skill with proficiency after simply hearing you talk about it. If participants do not have the opportunity to practice new strategies in a risk-free environment (Wycoff et al., 2003), the likelihood that the strategy will actually make it into the classroom is relatively low.

> **KEEP YOUR OWN LEARNING NEEDS IN MIND WHEN SELECTING PROFESSIONAL LEARNING.**

Finally, consider the format of the professional learning. Is it a workshop . . . online learning . . . a conference session . . . a professional learning community (PLC)? In which format do you learn best? Keep your own learning needs in mind when selecting professional learning. Also think about whether or not the activity will allow teachers the opportunity for collaboration, follow-up, and feedback (DeMonte, 2013). Learners need time to digest, reflect and connect personally to the content in order for the professional learning to make the desired impact (Wycoff et al., 2003). Think about some of the more effective professional learning experiences that you have had. They likely engaged you through introducing relevant skills and strategies, provided a chance to think about real application in your classroom, gave participants an opportunity to practice, and encouraged reflection and feedback from other teachers. Perhaps this was through a book study or online coursework, and this best fit your learning needs. Professional learning that engages you in the ways in which you learn best and facilitates an atmosphere of collaboration will likely have the most significant impact on your classroom and your professional growth.

All of the information outlined here may not be immediately evident in a session or workshop description. If this is the case and you have time, contact the facilitator for additional information. Most professional learning leaders will be happy to share additional information with you. When deciding on learning opportunities, look through the lens of, "How will this affect my classroom?" Keeping this at the forefront of your decision making will help in a couple of ways. First, it will support student growth and development. If talent development is the goal, getting the knowledge and skills to reach this goal should be your main focus in selecting professional learning. Learning that can be implemented in the classroom and help your students has the biggest and most significant impact. As a result of this learning, the change you effect in the classroom will also build your professional knowledge and expertise. You will not grow in your craft or become an expert through doing the same thing, over and over. You develop through being up-to-date on relevant educational information, trying and evaluating new things, and reflecting on successes and failures. In this way, you increase your knowledge and resources and move from being novice toward becoming an expert.

Figure 4 is a professional learning checklist for your use.

Professional Learning Checklist

Yes	No	
❑	❑	Will this professional learning make a significant change to my students' learning?
❑	❑	Is the facilitator someone with recent, practical experience related to the topic?
❑	❑	Will I be able to implement the knowledge and skills immediately in my classroom?
❑	❑	Will I have an opportunity to practice new strategies?
❑	❑	Will I have an opportunity to collaborate with other teachers?
❑	❑	Is the format of the professional learning best for my learning needs?

Figure 4. Professional learning checklist.

BUILDING A PERSONAL LEARNING NETWORK

Professional learning happens in a variety of ways. Yes, there are classes, workshops, PLCs, and the like. However, you can maximize your capacity for ongoing learning through the establishment of a personal learning network (PLN). A PLN is a system of constantly evolving connections and resources that support informal learning (Trust, Krutka, & Carpenter, 2016). Personal learning networks can include collaborative partnerships with other schools or universities; teacher colearning (Avalos, 2011); online resources such as social media, blogs, and podcasts; and participation in state or local gifted organizations. In a PLN, communication is ongoing and systems evolve organically.

Teachers who develop and actively participate in PLNs benefit in a variety of ways. Not only do you gain resources and systems for feedback, but also PLNs support your social, affective, intellectual, and identity needs as a teacher. Teachers who participate in PLNs frequently modify their teaching practices as a direct result of their learning. These teachers can see a positive impact on their students' learning, based on the knowledge and skills developed through this network. Teachers may even change the way teachers think about teaching (Trust et al., 2016). Today, educators have the benefit of immediate connection, answers, and feedback via technology. Imagine sitting at your desk at the end of a particularly difficult day and not knowing how in the world you can fix what went poorly in class today. Reaching out via social media to your PLN will likely yield answers and strategies that you hadn't thought of, and it may very well also validate your doubts and frustrations. You have a whole cohort of supporters on your phone! A podcast that you listen to on the way to work may give you an idea or resource for teaching something in a new way that same morning. This on-the-fly learning has the potential to make a significant impact on your professional knowledge and skill set.

Begin establishing a PLN through developing a professional presence on social media platforms, subscribing to relevant and well-informed blogs of other practitioners in the field, reaching out to local or remote university programs to make contact with other experts in the field of gifted education, and joining your local state or national gifted organization. Subscribe to podcasts and newsletters from professional organizations and individuals. Take part in scheduled online conversations about gifted education. Even dipping your toe into one or two of these suggestions will yield a huge return of other resources from which you can learn. Technology gives us the capacity to engage on a much wider scale than just our campus or district. Leveraging these tools appropriately can provide you with a rich community of individuals, organizations, and resources that will help you grow professionally.

WHAT A PLN IS NOT

When identifying people and resources to add to your PLN, please keep professional appropriateness at the center of your selection. Personal learning networks are not avenues for you to vent your frustrations or complain. This is not solution-focused behavior; this is just a negative online teachers' lounge. If you are seeking solutions to a problem, be factual, solution-oriented, and open to new ideas. Useful and productive PLNs include others from the gifted education field who have different ideas and approaches, different student demographics, and different resources. You do not stand to learn much if you surround yourself with other teachers just like you. A homogeneous PLN can quickly devolve into bad habits reinforcing themselves, and very little positivity. Teaching is hard enough. You do not need extra negativity.

Professional learning networks are also not platforms to make money or simply purchase the work of others. Can you use a PLN to collaborate and share lessons and resources? Absolutely. But establishing a PLN just to buy ready-made lessons or make extra money misses the point. Sharing with other great teachers is a valuable opportunity to grow and can be a great platform for ongoing collaboration. Use your PLN to engage with others in the spirit of learning and reciprocity, not simply as a quick way to get a cute activity for class tomorrow.

When selecting people, organizations, and resources to add to your PLN, look for quality indicators. For example, you can look toward major figures in the field to see who they follow and which organizational affiliations they support. Try to include resources that use facts, best practices, and research as the basis for their ideas and opinions. Get ideas and feedback from others, but make sure that the others in your network are giving you quality information. Be wary of resources that may present conflicting information, do not seem based in fact, or are out-of-touch with current education practices.

When engaging with social media, remember that whatever presence you develop online is permanent and out there for the whole world to see. Social

> **WHEN YOU GROW YOURSELF, YOU ARE ABLE TO MORE SUCCESSFULLY GROW YOUR STUDENTS.**

media platforms can provide quick, informal, brainstorming-style access to other educators and professionals, and this is an invaluable resource. You can take part in conversations that help you grow and think about topics in new and different ways. However, oversharing or presenting information that paints your school or students in a negative light is problematic. Be respectful of others, do not engage in an exchange that looks like it is taking a negative turn, and think about whether or not the things you put out into the ether might be taken the wrong way.

You want to create a PLN profile that mirrors what you would present on a resume. Remember, this is an opportunity for professional learning and growth. Protect your reputation, online and in person (Forbes, 2017) by carefully considering how you present yourself. You may share information about yourself that includes your background, your interests, things you would like to learn more about, and personal facts that lend themselves to an overall professional view of you. When you engage with this persona, you are putting your best learning, growing, teaching self into the world. You will get back what you put out, so make sure it is quality. A PLN is an invaluable resource for any teacher. Creating a virtual network of others in the field of gifted education can do quite a bit to ease that feeling of being on an island, and can provide on-demand support and resources. This is a great practice for ensuring continual professional development.

Professional learning and development is key in staying on top of best practices, new ideas, research, and resources in any field. As gifted education continues to evolve and become more inclusive, teachers must do so too in order to stay current. Relevant and responsive educators select professional learning carefully so as to use their time wisely and leverage their peers through a variety of PLN structures. When you grow yourself, you can more successfully grow your students. Do not neglect this important part of being an educator. Often, we find ourselves bogged down by the day-to-day demands of school. Making professional growth a priority helps us to move out of our ruts, keeps us fresh, and makes that day-to-day easier. Being a gifted teacher is filled with ups and downs, uncertainties, and sometimes unsure next steps. Use professional learning as an opportunity to surround yourself with experts and peers who will lift you up through collaboration, honest reflection, and a willingness to always help with that next step forward.

References

Amend, E. R., & Peters, D. (2015). The role of clinical psychologist: Building a comprehensive understanding of 2e students. *Gifted Child Today, 38,* 243–245. doi:10.1177/1076217515597286

American School Counselor Association. (2017). *ASCA position statements.* Retrieved from https://www.schoolcounselor.org/asca/media/asca/PositionStatements/PositionStatements.pdf

Assouline, S. G., & Whiteman, C. S., (2011). Twice-exceptionality: Implications for school psychologists in the post-IDEA 2004 era. *Journal of Applied School Psychology, 27,* 380–402.

Avalos, B. (2011). Teacher professional development in teaching and teacher education over ten years. *Teaching and Teacher Education, 27*(1), 10–20.

Briggs, C. J., Reis, S. M., & Sullivan, E. E. (2008). A national view of promising programs and practices for culturally, linguistically, and ethnically diverse gifted and talented students. *Gifted Child Quarterly, 52,* 131–145. doi:10.1177/0016986208316037

Buhl, H. M., & Hilkenmeier, J. (2017). Professionalism in parent-teacher conversations: Aspects, determinants, and consequences. A competence-oriented discussion. *Journal for Educational Research Online, 9,* 102–113.

Callahan, C. M., Moon, T. R., & Oh, S. (2017). Describing the status of programs for the gifted: A call for action. *Journal for the Education of the Gifted, 40,* 20–49. doi:10.1177/016235 3216686215

Chandler, K. L., (2012). Science curriculum for the gifted: Innovations for meeting student needs. *Japan Society for Science Education, 36,* 113–121. doi:10.14935/jssej.36.113

Clinkenbeard, P. R. (2012). Motivation and gifted students: Implications of theory and research. *Psychology in the Schools, 49,* 622–630. doi:10.1002/pits.21628

Colangelo, N., Assouline, S. G., & Gross, M. U. M. (Eds.). (2004). *A nation deceived: How schools hold back America's brightest students* (Vol. 2). Iowa City: The University of Iowa, The Connie Belin & Jacqueline N. Blank International Center for Gifted Education and Talent Development.

Coleman, M. R., & Gallagher, S. (2015). Meeting the needs of students with 2e: It takes a team. *Gifted Child Today, 38,* 252. doi:10.1177/1076217515597274

Cross, T. L. (2009). Social and emotional development of gifted children: Straight talk. *Gifted Child Today, 32*(2), 40.

Dai, D. Y., & Chen, F. (2013). Three paradigms of gifted education: In search of conceptual clarity in research and practice. *Gifted Child Quarterly, 57,* 151–168. doi:10.1177/0016986213490020

Dai, D. Y., Moon, S. M., & Feldhusen, J. F. (1998). Achievement motivation and gifted students: A social cognitive perspective. *Educational Psychologist, 33,* 45–63. doi:10.1080/00461520.19 98.9653290

DeMonte, J. (2013). *High-quality professional development for teachers: Supporting teacher training to improve student learning.* Washington, DC: Center for American Progress.

de Wet, C. F., & Gubbins, E. J. (2011). Teachers' beliefs about culturally, linguistically, and economically diverse gifted students: A quantitative study. *Roeper Review, 33,* 97–108. doi:10.1080/ 02783193.2011.554157

Dinnocenti, S. T. (1998, Spring). Differentiation: Definition and description for gifted and talented. *The National Research Center on the Gifted and Talented Newsletter,* 10–11.

Foley-Nicpon, M., Assouline, S. G., & Colangelo, N. (2013). Twice-exceptional learners: Who needs to know what? *Gifted Child Quarterly, 57,* 169–180. doi:10.1177/0016986213490021

Forbes, D. (2017). Professional online presence and learning networks: Educating for ethical use of social media. *International Review of Research in Open and Distance Learning, 18,* 175–190.

Gagné, F. (1985). Giftedness and talent: Reexamining a reexamination of the definitions. *Gifted Child Quarterly, 29,* 103–112.

Gardner, H. (1983). *Frames of mind: The theory of multiple intelligences.* New York, NY: Basic Books.

Gardner, H. (1993). *Frames of mind: The theory of multiple intelligences* (10th anniversary ed.). New York, NY: Basic Books.

Garet, M. S., Porter, A. C., Desimone, L., Birman, B. F., & Yoon, K. S. (2001). What makes professional development effective? Results from a national sample of teachers. *American Educational Research Journal, 38,* 915–945.

Gavin, M. K., Casa, T. M., Adelson, J. L., Carroll, S. R., & Sheffield, L. J. (2009). The impact of advanced curriculum on the achievement of mathematically promising elementary students. *Gifted Child Quarterly, 53,* 188–202. doi:10.1177/0016986209334964

Hains, S. J., Gross, J. M. S., Blue-Banning, M., Francis, G. L., & Turnbull, A. P. (2015). Fostering family–school and community–school partnerships in inclusive schools: Using practice as a guide. *Research and Practice for Persons with Severe Disabilities, 40,* 227–239. doi:10.1177/1540796915594141

Hockett, J. A. (2009). Curriculum for highly able learners that conforms to general education and gifted education quality indicators. *Journal for the Education of the Gifted, 32,* 394–440. doi:10.4219/jeg-2009-857

Johnsen, S. K. (2013). National challenges in providing services to gifted students. *Gifted Child Today, 36*(1), 5–6. doi:10.1177/1076217512468415

Johnsen, S. K., & Clarenbach, J. (Eds.). (2017). *Using the national gifted education standards for pre-k–grade 12 professional development* (2nd ed.). Waco, TX: Prufrock Press.

Kennedy, K., & Farley, J. (2018). Counseling gifted students: School-based considerations and strategies. *International*

Electronic Journal of Elementary Education, 10, 361–367. doi:10.26822/iejee.2018336194

Kim, M. (2016). A meta-analysis of the effects of enrichment programs on gifted students. *Gifted Child Quarterly, 60,* 102–116. doi:10.1177/0016986216630607

Kitsantas, A., Bland, L., & Chirinos, D. S. (2017). Gifted students' perceptions of gifted programs: An inquiry into their academic and social-emotional functioning. *Journal for the Education of the Gifted, 40,* 266–288.

Kronholz, J. (2016). Teacher home visits: School-family partnerships foster student success. *Education Next, 16*(3), 16.

Kulik, C.-L. C., Kulik, J. A., & Bangert-Drowns, R. L. (1990). Effectiveness of mastery learning programs: A meta-analysis. *Review of Educational Research, 60,* 265–299. https://doi.org/10.3102/00346543060002265

Lawson, G. M., McKenzie, M. E., Becker, K. D., Selby, L., & Hoover, S. A. (2019). The core components of evidence-based social emotional learning programs. *Prevention Science, 20,* 457–467. doi:10.1007/s11121-018-0953-y

Lin, M., & Bates, A. B. (2010). Home visits: How do they affect teachers' beliefs about teaching and diversity? *Early Childhood Education Journal, 38,* 179–185. doi:10.1007/s10643-010-0393-1

Little, C. A., Feng, A. X., VanTassel-Baska, J., Rogers, K. B., & Avery, L. D. (2007). A study of curriculum effectiveness in social studies. *Gifted Child Quarterly, 51,* 272–284. doi:10.1177/0016986207302722

Lopez, S. J., & Louis, M. C. (2009). The principles of strengths-based education. *Journal of College and Character, 10*(4).

Makel, M. C., Snyder, K. E., Thomas, C., Malone, P. S., & Putallaz, M. (2015). Gifted students' implicit beliefs about intelligence and giftedness. *Gifted Child Quarterly, 59,* 203–212. doi:10.1177/0016986215599057

Marland, S. P., Jr. (1972). *Education of the gifted and talented: Report to the Congress of the United States by the U.S. Commissioner of Education and background papers submitted to the U.S. Office of Education,* 2 vols. Washington, DC: U.S. Government Printing Office. (Government Documents, Y4.L 11/2: G36)

McGee, C. D., & Hughes, C. E. (2011). Identifying and supporting young gifted learners. *YC Young Children, 66*(4), 100.

McHatton, P. A., Boyer, N. R., Shaunessy, E., Terry, P. M., & Farmer, J. L. (2010). Principals' perceptions of preparation and practice in gifted and special education content: Are we doing enough? *Journal of Research on Leadership Education, 5,* 1-22. doi:10.1177/194277511000500101

Minke, K. M., Sheridan, S. M., Kim, E. M., Ryoo, J. H., & Koziol, N. A. (2014). Congruence in parent-teacher relationships: The role of shared perceptions. *The Elementary School Journal, 114,* 527–546. doi:10.1086/675637

Morawska, A., & Sanders, M. R. (2008). Parenting gifted and talented children: What are the key child behaviour and parenting issues? *Australasian Psychiatry, 42,* 819–827. doi:10.1080/00048670802277271

Nathan, L. (2015). The art of the school-community partnership: Successful partnerships require careful attention and oversight, but they can change both schools and their partners and offer new resources and opportunities to students. *Phi Delta Kappan, 96*(8), 57.

National Association for Gifted Children, (n.d.-a). *Myths about gifted students.* Retrieved from: https://www.nagc.org/myths-about-gifted-students

National Association for Gifted Children, (n.d.-b). *Theoretical frameworks for giftedness.* Retrieved from: https://www.nagc.org/theoretical-frameworks-giftedness

National Association for Gifted Children, & The Association for the Gifted, Council for Exceptional Children. (2013). *NAGC-CEC teacher preparation standards in gifted education.* Retrieved from http://www.nagc.org/sites/default/files/standards/NAGC-%20CEC%20CAEP%20standards%20%282013%20final%29.pdf

National Education Association. (2006). *The twice-exceptional dilemma.* Washington, DC: Author.

Neihart, M., Pfeiffer, S. I., & Cross, T. L. (Eds.) (2016). *The social and emotional development of gifted children: What do we know?* (2nd ed.). Waco, TX: Prufrock Press.

Nzinga-Johnson, S., Baker, J. A., & Aupperlee, J. (2009). Teacher-parent relationships and school involvement among racially and educationally diverse parents of kindergartners. *The Elementary School Journal, 110*(1), 81–91.

Omdal, S. (2015). Twice exceptionality from a practitioner's perspective. *Gifted Child Today, 38,* 246.

Page, A. (2006). Three models for understanding gifted education. *Kairaranga, 7*(2), 11–15.

Penney, S., & Wilgosh, L. (2000). Fostering parent-teacher relationships when children are gifted. *Gifted Education International, 14,* 217–229.

Pfeiffer S. I., & Blei, S. (2008). Gifted identification beyond the IQ test: Rating scales and other assessment procedures. In S. I. Pfeiffer (Ed.), *Handbook of giftedness in children: Psychoeducational theory, research, and best practices* (pp. 177–198). New York, NY: Springer Science + Business Media.

Pierson, E. E., Kilmer, L. M., Rothlisberg, B. A., & McIntosh, D. E. (2012). Use of brief intelligence tests in the identification of giftedness. *Journal of Psychoeducational Assessment, 30,* 10–24. doi:10.1177/0734282911428193

Plucker, J. A., & Barab, S. A. (2005). The importance of contexts in theories of giftedness: Learning to embrace the messy joys of subjectivity. In R. J. Sternberg & J. E. Davidson (Eds.), *Conceptions of giftedness* (2nd ed., pp. 201–216). New York, NY: Cambridge University Press.

Plucker, J. A., & Callahan, C. M. (2014). Research on giftedness and gifted education: Status of the field and considerations for the future. *Exceptional Children, 80,* 390–406.

Reis, S. M., Baum, S. M., & Burke, E. (2014). An operational definition of twice-exceptional learners: Implications and applications. *Gifted Child Quarterly, 58,* 217–230. https://doi.org/10.1177/0016986214534976

Reis, S. M., & Renzulli, J. S. (2004). Current research on the social and emotional development of gifted and talented students: Good news and future possibilities. *Psychology in the Schools, 41,* 119–130. doi:10.1002/pits.10144

Reis, S. M., & Renzulli, J. S. (2009). The schoolwide enrichment model: A focus on student strengths and interests. In J. S.

Renzulli, E. J. Gubbins, K. S. McMillen, R. D. Eckert, & C. A. Little (Eds.), *Systems and models for developing programs for the gifted and talented* (2nd ed., pp. 323–352). Waco, TX: Prufrock Press.

Reis, S. M., & Westberg, K. L. (1994). The impact of staff development on teachers' ability to modify curriculum for gifted and talented students. *Gifted Child Quarterly, 38,* 127–135.

Renzulli, J. S. (1978). What makes giftedness? Re-examining a definition. *Phi Delta Kappa, 60,* 180–181.

Renzulli, J. S., & Reis, S. M. (2014). *The schoolwide enrichment model: A how-to guide for talent development* (3rd ed.). Waco, TX: Prufrock Press.

Roberts, S. M., & Lovett, S. B. (1994). Examining the "F" in gifted: Academically gifted adolescents' physiological and affective responses to scholastic failure. *Journal for the Education of the Gifted, 17,* 241–259. doi:10.1177/016235329401700304

Rogers, K. B. (2007). Lessons learned about educating the gifted and talented: A synthesis of the research on educational practice. *Gifted Child Quarterly, 51,* 382–396. doi:10.1177/0016986207306324

Rosenfield, S., & Houtz, J. C. (1978). Developmental patterns in problem solving and divergent thinking abilities in gifted elementary school children. *Journal for the Education of the Gifted, 1*(2), 37–48. doi:10.1177/016235327800100207

Rotigel, J. V. (2003). Understanding the young gifted child: Guidelines for parents, families and educators. *Early Childhood Education Journal, 30,* 209–214.

Rubenstein, L. D., & Ridgley, L. M. (2017). Unified program design: Organizing existing programming models, delivery options, and curriculum. *Gifted Child Today, 40,* 163–174. doi:10.1177/1076217517707234

Rule, A. C., & Montgomery, S. E. (2013). Using cartoons to teach about perfectionism: Supporting gifted students' social-emotional development. *Gifted Child Today, 36,* 255–262. doi:10.1177/1076217513497574

Salmela, M., & Määttä, K. (2015). Even the best have difficulties: A study of Finnish straight-A graduates' resource-oriented solutions. *Gifted Child Quarterly, 59*, 124–135. doi:10.1177/0016986214568720

Selecting curricula for gifted programs. (2004). *Gifted Child Today, 27*(3), 8.

Shaunessy, E. (2003). State policies regarding gifted education. *Gifted Child Today, 26*(3), 16–65. https://doi.org/10.4219/gct-2003-103

Siegle, D. (2013). *The underachieving gifted child: Recognizing, understanding, and reversing underachievement.* Waco, TX: Prufrock Press.

Siegle, D., & McCoach, D. B. (2005). Making a difference: Motivating gifted students who are not achieving. *Teaching Exceptional Children, 38*(1), 22–27.

Silverman, L. K. (1997). The construct of asynchronous development. *Peabody Journal of Education, 72*, 36–58. doi:10.1080/0161956X.1997.9681865

Silverman, L. K. (2009). The two-edged sword of compensation: How the gifted cope with learning disabilities. *Gifted Education International, 25*, 115–130. doi:10.1177/026142940902500203

Smith, M. M., Saklofske, D. H., Stoeber, J., & Sherry, S. B. (2016). The big three perfectionism scale: A new measure of perfectionism. *Journal of Psychoeducational Assessment, 34*, 670–687. doi:10.1177/0734282916651539

Sriraman, B. (2004). Gifted ninth graders' notions of proof: Investigating parallels in approaches of mathematically gifted students and professional mathematicians. *Journal for the Education of the Gifted, 27*, 267–292.

Stambaugh T. (2010, April). *Curriculum and instructional strategies for promising students of poverty* [Webinar]. Washington, DC: National Association for Gifted Children.

Stanley, N. V. (1993). Gifted and the "Zone of Proximal Development." *Gifted Education International, 9*, 78–80. https://doi.org/10.1177/026142949300900203

Sternberg, R. J. (1999). The theory of successful intelligence. *Review of General Psychology, 3*, 292–316. doi:10.1037//1089-2680.3.4.292

Subotnik, R. F., Olszewski-Kubilius, P., & Worrell, F. C. (2011). Rethinking giftedness and gifted education: A proposed direction forward based on psychological science. *Psychological Science in the Public Interest, 12*(1), 3–54. doi:10.1177/1529100611418056

Sullivan, A. L. (2011). Disproportionality in special education identification and placement of English language learners. *Exceptional Children, 77,* 317–334. doi:10.1177/00144029 1107700304

Swanson, J. D. (2016). Drawing upon lessons learned: effective curriculum and instruction for culturally and linguistically diverse gifted learners. *Gifted Child Quarterly, 60,* 172–191. https://doi. org/10.1177/0016986216642016

Texas Education Agency. (2019). *Gifted talented education.* Retrieved from https://tea.texas.gov/academics/special_student _populations/gifted_and_talented_education_gifted_talented_ education

Tomlinson, C. A. (2008). The goals of differentiation. *Educational Leadership, 66,* 26–30.

Tomlinson, C. A., & Jarvis, J. M. (2014). Case studies of success: Supporting academic success for students with high potential from ethnic minority and economically disadvantaged backgrounds. *Journal for the Education of the Gifted, 37,* 191–219.

Tomlinson, C. A., Kaplan, S. N., Renzulli, J. S., Purcell, J., Leppien, J., & Burns, D. (2002). *The parallel curriculum: A design to develop high potential and challenge high-ability learners.* Washington, DC: National Association for Gifted Children.

Trust, T., Krutka, D. G., & Carpenter, J. P. (2016). "Together we are better": Professional learning networks for teachers. *Computers & Education, 102,* 15. doi:10.1016/j.compedu.2016.06.007

van Rossum, J. H. A., & Gagné, F. (2006). Talent development in sports. In F. A. Dixon & S. M. Moon (Eds.), *The handbook of secondary gifted education* (p. 283). Waco, TX: Prufrock Press.

VanTassel-Baska, J. (1998). *Planning science programs for high ability learners.* ERIC Digest E546.

VanTassel-Baska, J. (2003). What matters in curriculum for gifted learners: Reflections on theory, research, and practice. In N. Colangelo & G. A. Davis (Eds.), *Handbook of gifted education* (3rd ed., pp. 174–183). Boston, MA: Pearson.

VanTassel-Baska, J. (2015). Curriculum issues: Error analysis in thinking about curriculum for the gifted. *Gifted Child Today, 38,* 198–199. doi:10.1177/1076217515583746

VanTassel-Baska, J. (2017). Curriculum issues: The importance of selecting literature for gifted learners. *Gifted Child Today, 40,* 183–184. doi:10.1177/1076217517713783

VanTassel-Baska, J., & Brown, E. F. (2007). Toward best practice: An analysis of the efficacy of curriculum models in gifted education. *Gifted Child Quarterly, 51,* 342–358. doi:10.1177/0016986207306323

VanTassel-Baska, J., & Wood, S. (2010). The integrated curriculum model (ICM). *Learning and individual differences, 20,* 345–357.

Wang, C. W., & Neihart, M. (2015). Academic self-concept and academic self-efficacy: Self-beliefs enable academic achievement of twice-exceptional students. *Roeper Review, 37,* 63–73. doi:10.1080/02783193.2015.1008660

Weber, C. L., & Stanley, L. (2012). Educating parents of gifted children. *Gifted Child Today, 35,* 128.

Welter, M. M., Jaarsveld, S., & Lachmann, T. (2018). Problem space matters: Evaluation of a German enrichment program for gifted children. *Frontiers in Psychology, 9,* 569. doi:10.3389/fpsyg.2018.00569

Westberg, K. L., Burns, D. E., Gubbins, E. J., Reis, S. M., Park, S., & Maxfield, L. R. (1998). *Professional development practices in gifted education: Results of a national survey.* (ERIC Document Reproduction Service No. 424708)

Whiteman, J. (2013). Connecting with families: Tips for those difficult conversations. *Young Children, 68,* 94–95.

Willard-Holt, C., Weber, J., Morrison, K. L., & Horgan, J. (2013). Twice-exceptional learners' perspectives on effective learning strategies. *Gifted Child Quarterly, 57,* 247–262. https://doi.org/10.1177/0016986213501076

Wiskow, K., Fowler, V. D., & Christopher, M. M. (2011). Active advocacy: Working together for appropriate services for gifted learners. *Gifted Child Today, 34,* 20–25. doi:10.1177/107621751103400207

Wood, S. (2010). Best practices in counseling the gifted in schools: What's really happening? *Gifted Child Quarterly, 54,* 42.

Woods, J. (2016). *State and federal policy: Gifted and talented youth.* Retrieved from http://www.ecs.org/wp-content/uploads/State_and_Federal_Policy_for_Gifted_and_Talented_Youth.pdf

Wycoff, M., Nash, W. R., Juntune, J. E., & Mackay, L. (2003). Purposeful professional development: Planning positive experiences for teachers of the gifted and talented. *Gifted Child Today, 26*(4), 34–64. doi:10.4219/gct-2003-116

Young, M. H., & Balli, S. J. (2014). Gifted and talented education (GATE): Student and parent perspectives. *Gifted Child Today, 37,* 236–246. doi:10.1177/1076217514544030

ABOUT THE AUTHOR

Kari Lockhart has worked in education for 10 years and has spent a significant portion of that time in the gifted field. She has been a classroom English language arts teacher, gifted and talented teacher, campus administrator, campus gifted coordinator, English language arts instructional coach, and district gifted and talented coordinator. Kari received her undergraduate degree from Austin College and her graduate degree from the University of North Texas. She is currently a doctoral student studying educational psychology with a focus on gifted and talented populations at the University of North Texas. She hopes to be able enjoy a lifelong career in education and be an advocate for gifted students and their families.

Printed in the United States
by Baker & Taylor Publisher Services